Bridging True Love Connection & Healing Between You and Your Animals

HEALING YOU, HEALING YOUR ANIMAL

Vicki Draper

Vi Miere
Bothell, Washington

Author: Vicki Draper

Publisher: Vi Miere, Bothell, Washington

Website: HealingYourAnimal.com

Photos: by Jill Labberton with Lifestyle Portraits unless otherwise stated

Editing and Layout: Amy Collette

Cover Design: Robin Kerr

Healing Your Animal: Bridging True Love Connection & Healing Between You and Your Animal/ Vicki Draper. —1st ed.

ISBN 978-0-9976350-0-3

Liliana,

It was nice meeting you
in class. My wish is that both
serve you and your animals
with health, harmony and ease!

Vicki

Foreword

For me, the quest to understand our animal friends, why they do what they do and how to resolve their behavior, training and healing issues has been a lifelong pursuit. From my earliest memories, animals have been my passion. Perhaps that had something to do with the fact that I always felt comfortable with animals but not so much with humans. Even though I grew up in a big-city environment, I lived with a variety of animals. It seemed like there was an invisible shingle above my door that said, "Any animals needing help, come here" and they did! I learned a lot from all of these animal friends of mine but not enough. I couldn't always save them all and this was difficult to accept. I began pursuing what would become my career path very early on. I trained my first dog in grade school. By the time I was a teenager I was apprenticing with professional trainers to learn more. When I was old enough, I got a job with the local veterinarian and worked in that field for almost twenty years, earning a degree in Veterinary Technology.

While working in veterinary medicine for all those years, I was also working as a dog trainer on my way to becoming an animal behavior therapist. Eventually, I realized that, what I now call the left-brain, scientific world of animal training and veterinary medicine was limited in providing me with the answers I was seeking to understand and help our animal friends. I had to move out of the square and into the right-brain, more subjective world of alternative medicine practices, metaphysics and spirituality.

This path did lead me to the answers I was seeking and what I now call the keys to understanding our animal friends. The most important here are interspecies telepathic and empathetic communication.

Later in my journey, I was fortunate to have a kindred spirit, Vicki Draper, cross my path. I believe that was more than ten years ago. She was working at a place where I was teaching my classes, doing massage therapy on animals. She attended my classes and I remember being very impressed with her. I really liked her energy and I could sense she had a gift when it came to healing animals. I was so impressed with her that I had her do some work on an unbalanced rescue dog of mine. Since that time, I have kept up with her career and work with animals. I have always believed that her crystal essences are amazing. Hers are the only crystal essences that I personally recommend to my clients.

Vicki is passionate about her work and has grown into an expert at healing animals. In her work she uses many modalities like massage, cranial sacral work, reiki and acupressure, along with her crystal essences. She also understands and uses interspecies telepathic communication. Because she understands the empathetic nature of animals and the fact that they take on and process their human's stuff, she includes working on and educating us humans in the work she does to heal our animals. She works in-person and remotely with many animals and their humans, as well as teaching classes.

I was very flattered when she asked if I would write a foreword for her new book. My intuition said to say yes, so I did. Simply reading the book made me feel better! Energetically this book is special. I believe this book has great benefit within it for not only your animal friends, but for you as well.

This book is intended to be a slow read and is a process that you will go through with your animal friends. Vicki recommends that you read each chapter in order and go through the process described in each chapter before moving on to the next. I agree that is how the book will be most helpful.

I am impressed by the simplicity of this book. It contains much wisdom without being overwhelming. In it, Vicki touches on the keys to understanding our animal friends. They are telepathic and empathetic communication and what I call the Human to Animal Transference (animals pick up, process and reflect back our belief systems, behavior, characteristics and especially our suppressed negative emotional energy.) She shares excellent tools to help you in both areas.

The biggest challenge I see with this book is that it is not a magic wand. It does require that you take the time to do the work. If you are up to the challenge, read and do the work, I believe this book will work magic. It will not only help you understand and be able to resolve many issues with and for your animal friends but it will heal you in that process! What a gift, indeed. Enjoy the journey...

Martha Norwalk
Animal behavior therapist, trainer and
host of Martha Norwalk's Animal World

Contents

Dedication

As I fulfill my lifelong dream of publishing a book, this book is dedicated to:

My daughter, Miranda, who is a delightful soul who also has the natural healing connections with animals (and people). She gets the benefit of receiving a language and support in using her gifts early in her life to be able to help many people and animals. I am grateful to be an example to her for following her heart and passions in life. She inspires me to be my best as a mother, as a person, and as a healer, helping many people and animals.

Miranda with Spirit and Sapphire

My Dad, Mom and Sister who have always supported me even when they may not have fully understood the depths of my communication and connection with animals.

Heron, who came to me on a nature walk when I was first preparing my eight-week training course that is the impetus for this book. The message Heron had for me was very loud and clear "Believe in yourself." When receiving Heron's message, the energy was so strong it nearly knocked me over. Which is ironic since Heron is about standing on your own two feet. I am so grateful for Heron's message that rocked me to my core to be here today delivering this book with valuable, proven techniques that will make a difference in your and your animal's quality of life.

Tasha, my "heart" cat who was totally by my side for over 19 years and all of my life's changes and transformations during this time. Little did I know the day I went to the pound and brought her home at seven weeks old what a journey we would embark on together. I am grateful for her inspiration to find the courage to branch out and serve many more people and animals with what she taught me in supporting her live a good quality of life during her time with me.

Spirit and Sapphire coming into my life now at four months old to bridge true love connection and healing with them at this time in my life.

And to all of the people and animals in my life who have benefitted from using these healing techniques that are now helping you have a deeper connection and healthier life with your animals.

How to Use This Book

You purchased this book with an intention. And with your intention, whether conscious or unconscious, you have activated a healing journey for you and your animals. In order to take your healing experience deeper, I invite you to clarify what you would like to receive and what benefit you desire from reading this book. Setting your intention is a powerful part of healing.

Setting intentions is key in working with energy. You are sending a request to the Universe and allowing it to respond to you with what you desire.

When I use the word Universe, it is interchangeable with the term you use for your Spiritual Source. It is what some call God, Source, Higher Self, Buddha, Guardian Angel, etc. So whatever that is for you, please use it in place of the word Universe in this book.

To get the most out of this journey with your animal, I encourage you to read this book from cover to cover, taking in the information and techniques and incorporating the ones you prefer. Each chapter builds on the one before it. This book takes you through the model of a healing session and puts it all together at the end. Then I invite you to go through this book again, starting with Chapter 1 and going through each chapter, taking the time to practice each chapter's teachings before going on to the next one.

After reading this book, it can then be a valuable resource to come back to in order to keep strengthening and cultivating your energy management, intuition, calming techniques, connection and healing with you and your animals.

The journey we are on for the next nine chapters is about deep connection and healing for both you and your animals. This book gives you a great foundation of energy management with grounding, clearing, and protecting, along with calming techniques, strengthening your intuition, learning basic animal communication, and the importance of assigning roles. Communication and connection happen on many levels.

Each chapter will have a healing activation before we dive into the new material. We are all connected, so when one person and animal shifts, we all do. This allows each of us to play a key role in raising the vibrations of our planet Earth.

Energy is everywhere and everything has energy. Even thoughts are energy. This is why intentions are very powerful. This is where creation and manifesting your desires into your world starts. And this goes for your connection with your animals and their optimal health.

This book is designed to support you and your animals physically, emotionally, behaviorally, mentally and spiritually.

When reading this book, be open to receiving information in new ways. You may find yourself all of a sudden having a "knowing," a feeling of oneness, openness and joy, or even clarity with more awareness of your surroundings and a deeper connection with your animals. Drink extra water, especially on days of reading this book and practicing the techniques. Working with energy goes deep like massage for the physical body. Drinking water supports hydrating and flushing out toxins removed during a session.

As you are practicing the techniques presented in this book, I invite you to pay attention to all areas of your life: your relationships, your sleep, your financial flow, your digestion, your energy level, basically the health of all areas of your life.

You may notice shifts in dogs from going after neighbors and barking a lot to being calm, settled and quiet. In cats, you may notice them going from not getting along to getting along with one another, and much more is possible, for your animals and yourself. One client was amazed by how working with these techniques opened her sex life with her husband. One client's business really took off. One client didn't know she could feel as good as she did. Be open - **anything is possible.**

Healing You, Healing Your Animal Essences

Animals and nature are passions of mine. Both are a big part of my teachings. Using nature's crystals and minerals, I have formulated two lines of natural healing essences called Healing You and Healing Your Animal Essences.

Throughout the book you will encounter Essence Experiences that explain how the vibrational support of an essence will deepen your experiences which bridge connection and healing between you and your animal.

When you are drawn to a particular essence or essences to use for you and your animals, I invite you to visit:

HealingYourAnimal.com/Products.php

You will start benefiting right away with their healing support.

You may have noticed your animals looking at you more intently after getting this book. They may have sensed the energies building for your time together.

Your animals are excited for you to be doing this journey.

Acupressure

As a certified animal acupressurist for large and small animals (and people), I incorporate some acupressure points for you and your animal's highest healing benefit.

With acupressure, you only need a light touch. Actually, the weight of a nickel is all you have to use to make a difference and engage the acupressure points.

I invite you to get a nickel and place it on your finger tip to feel the weight. I then invite you to place the nickel on the back of your hand to experience how it feels. Next place it in the palm of your hand and feel the weight of it. This will help you gauge your pressure when using the acupressure techniques.

Acupressure techniques use the tips of your fingers to engage each point.

Massage

As a licensed animal massage practitioner for large and small animals (and people), I incorporate the passive touch massage stroke for your and your animal's highest healing benefit.

With the passive touch massage stroke you will be learning, you will only need a light touch. A gentle touch while engaging your animal's body will stimulate the circulatory system, muscles and tissues for optimal health.

You are invited to participate by sharing your experiences on the Healing You, Healing Your Animal Facebook group as you read and do the techniques in this book.

CHAPTER 1

My Story

HI, I'M VICKI DRAPER, Healing Your Animal Expert. Since 1999, during the many years of my practice, I have been privileged to play a key part in the remarkable healing of multiple species including cats, dogs, horses and people.

I was just 11 years old when **my kitten was diagnosed with distemper and only given a week to live.** Rather than accept a tragic diagnosis, I intuitively began visualizing a long, healthy life for him. **My precious kitten lived a happy and active life for many more years!**

For many years I kept this gift private (while actually living a life of being a computer programmer!), but then in 1999 my soul could no longer take it and I could no longer suppress my gift. I knew animals were meant to be a larger part of my life, but I didn't know how. Then one day during a hike I found a heart-shaped rock – the top was white and the bottom was grey. And **I realized I had a choice:** which way was my heart going to go? To live a life of sharing my gift: the white light? Or a life of dying a slow death: the grey? I chose the light.

Since that decisive day I have worked with thousands of happy and loyal pet guardians and their veterinarians to bring to life similar experiences for people and their pets.

I have come to both understand and know that **I have a healing touch** that brings anxious animals to a place of calm, fearful animals are empowered to feel safe, rescued animals are enabled to release the old and embrace the new with comfort, injured animals (whether through accident or old age) go from limping and having low energy to walking normally – often with a new spring in their step! **I often hear from my clients with older animals, "My animal now acts 10 years younger."** And many of my clients actually have the opportunity to enjoy many more years with their pets as a result of our work together. Happy clients cry tears of joy when **once again they are able to hear the purrs, woofs and pitter-patter of healthy paws.**

I have been told I embody a remarkable combination of Sherlock Holmes-inspired investigative skill, Dr. Doolittle-like communication and connection with animals, and Fairy Godmother-like oversight and compassion.

Combining these skills, I have created this book for you to deepen your love and connection with your animal, bridging communication and increasing well-being for you and your animals for as long as you have together. Let's get started...

CHAPTER 2

Preparing You

MY INTENTION IS TO HELP YOU LEARN TECHNIQUES that will deepen your connection with yourself and with your animals. The first part is getting you ready.

Healing Activation: Grounding Cord Exercise

Sit or stand and feel your feet touching the floor beneath you. Take a moment and close your eyes. If you are not at a place where you can close your eyes, pretend or imagine you can.

Take a moment and check in with how you are feeling at this moment. What is going on in your body? What is going on in your head? Are you feeling disconnected or scattered? Are you feeling centered and clear? No judgment, just notice. Do you feel floaty? Do you feel heavy energetically? Again, no judgment, just notice.

Now, pay attention to your feet. Take a moment to feel a very solid connection with the floor. I invite you to begin moving, rocking forwards and backwards on your feet while standing on the floor. Raise up your heels and stand on the balls of your feet. Now lower your heels and raise your toes up in the air while resting on the heels of your feet. Now do this a couple more times back and forth, to really get a good feel of your feet connecting with the floor. Do this a few times. And as your awareness is going to the ground with your focus on your feet on the floor, take a moment and feel that connection.

Now, feel the connection of your feet resting flat on the floor. Feel the connection of your feet going down through the floor and sensing the Earth underneath. As your feet are connecting to the Earth underneath your floor and you feel the Earth, (going through floors between you and the Earth if needed) see your grounding cord coming out from the center of your root chakra (base of your spine) and going down through the floor, through the Earth, all the way down to the center of the Earth. If you are unsure where your grounding cord is, it comes out of your body at your perineum, which is located between your vagina for females/your scrotum for males and your anus. If you are unable to see or feel this, pretend or imagine you can.

You are taking the end of it and pulling it down, all the way down to the center of the Earth. And on your way down to the center of the Earth, imagine putting some stakes hooking your cord into the Earth as you go down, so if it comes untethered at the core, you are still down into the Earth and can easily get back down to full grounding. And as your grounding cord is going down and hooking into the Earth and then going down farther and hooking into the Earth and going down farther and hooking into the Earth and going down farther and hooking into the Earth and continuing all the way down to the center of the Earth, where you can hook in and wrap your grounding cord around the core of the Earth. There is a ball of light, a core of light. So keep going down deep until you reach this light. This light feeds your grounding cord. Now take a moment and feel how this feels. Feel your deep connection with the Earth, your solid connection. Your feet and legs feel grounded, solid and stable. Now put your attention back on your grounding cord all the way in the center of the Earth, deeply connected to the Earth. Knowing this is what deep grounding is. Take a moment and sense how this feels. Sense how you feel, how your body feels. Sense how deep grounding feels to you.

This is now in your cellular memory. You always have this with you. When you are feeling a little off or ungrounded, you can remember this activation and easily get back to this feeling. Take another moment and really embrace how this feels. Do you notice a difference in how you feel now than when we started this grounding activation? How so? What is different now? This information will help you. Remember this grounded feeling.

You can open your eyes.

THERE ARE FIVE KEY ENERGY STEPS YOU WILL
RECEIVE IN THIS CHAPTER.

Each of the Five Key Energy Steps corresponds with a Healing You Essence that make up the Energy Essentials Essence
Package. If you are a person who likes the full experience,
you are invited to receive the Energy Essentials Essence
Package to use as you are going through the processes and
techniques in this book:

HealingYourAnimal.com/Products.php

Step 1: Grounding

You received grounding in the healing activation. Grounding
yourself is a key step in setting up your Animal Connection
and Healing session with your animal.

The more grounded and calm you feel, the calmer and more
grounded your animal will feel.

Now, you may be saying... Grounding?

What is grounding?

As a licensed animal massage practitioner, certified animal
acupressurist, Reiki master, and having a very special gift
with communicating and healing animals, what you may not
know is I also have a science background where I have de-
grees in computer science, math and physics.

According to physics, the definition of grounding is: the process of *removing* the excess charge on an object by means of
the transfer of electrons between it (in this case you, your
emotions) and another object of substantial size (in this case
the Earth).

An example of the positive charge is an excessively happy,
over-the-top ecstatic person, charged with enthusiasm. An

example of the negative charge is a very nervous, very fearful person, charged with fear and anxiety.

Grounding is great support, especially for you multi-taskers. When you have lots going on in your head and lots of energy, grounding will help you be clearer, more focused and calmer doing your multi-tasking, and you will be more efficient.

Here are some ways for you to ground:

a. One way is having your grounding cord connect to the center of the Earth (as you just experienced in the activation exercise). I find this technique easy because I can do it anywhere I am and at any time.

b. Taking a walk is grounding. I recommend a 20-minute walk outside at a minimum. This also helps boost your immune system.

c. Walk barefoot on the Earth – in the grass or dirt. (Not on a sidewalk that is manmade). You can even do this in the fallen leaves, dew or snow to feel all seasons of the Earth.

d. Food can be grounding. Beef, carrots, almonds, even chocolate are some common foods to help with grounding.

When you ground, you are not only calming yourself to feel safer and more secure, you are helping your animal feel safer and more secure.

❧ Your Essence Experience ❧

For extra support, the Healing You Ground essence is a simple, effective, easy-to-use way to ground. Simply spray the essence three times in the air around you to receive grounding support.

Step 2: Getting Present/Centering

This is where as humans, we have to do an extra step. Animals are always present. They are always in the here and now. As people, we tend to get caught up in the past or the future and need the reminder to be present.

There is a difference in being grounded and being present. I find the best way is to experience it. You just did a grounding exercise in the healing activation. So take a moment, check in and pay attention to how you feel.

Now, let's take a deep breath in, hold it, let it out. Take another deep breath in, hold it, let it out. And now for the power of three, take a deep breath in, hold it, let it out.

Now, check in and see how you feel. Can you feel a difference from just a moment ago before you took your three deep breaths? Is there more of an opening? More clarity? More awareness? More brightness? There is no right or wrong. Notice what it is for you.

❧ *Your Essence Experience* ❧

*For extra support, the Healing You **Iceland Spar** essence is a simple, effective, easy-to-use way to center. Simply spray the essence three times in the air around you to get present and receive centering support. I invite you to take a deep breath in and let it out now after spraying the essence. I find this helps the essence integrate even deeper.*

Step 3: Clearing You

You may be asking - What am I clearing?

And why is this so important?

You have a physical body and an energy body. You know what your physical body is, since you can see it, feel it and touch it. You (and your animals) also have an energy body that most people cannot see or feel, but it is real, it does exist, and it needs attention and care to maintain the state of its health to support the health of your physical body. Did you know most disease starts in the energy body? When not cleared, the disease eventually goes into the physical body.

Clearing your energy field regularly is an important step in maintaining optimum health, not only for you, but for your animals too.

When you are not clearing, on some level you are creating energetic clutter or chaos. In the same way you can have physical clutter, you can have energetic clutter.

I know this to be true first hand.

Vicki and Tasha
Photo by Zachary Folk – Folk Photography

My own cat, Tasha, lived to be 19 and always slept with me and was always near me. She was what I call my "heart cat." We had a very close and special relationship. She was with me as I worked from home and she would snuggle with me at night. She loved being with me. Any time I was not feeling well, she was by my side. When I let my life stresses build up and did not deal with them in a healthy way, she would quit sleeping with me and would throw up. I took her to the vet each time. After getting her checked out by the vet time and again, the vet would find nothing wrong. I finally realized it wasn't something physical. I learned that as soon as I would clear myself and clear her, she would stay healthy, be by my side and sleep with me again. She was a great teacher and a true barometer for me.

When you clear, you are introducing higher vibrations into your energy and your animal's energy field rather than con-tributing to and creating energetic clutter or chaos. You are bringing a peaceful energy to yourself and your animal.

Taking a shower helps clear your energy field. So when you are taking a shower, intend that your energy field is clearing as well as your physical body getting clean. Also use Healing You *Clear* essence to clear your energy field during the day.

❧ *Your Essence Experience* ❧

Healing You **Clear** *essence is a simple, effective, unscented, easy-to-use way to clear your energy field. Simply spray the essence three times in the air around you to receive clearing support and feel fresher. The* **Clear** *essence is a smokeless alternative to other clearing practices such as burning sage or palo santo wood, which can be harmful for people and animals with respiratory issues and compromised immune systems. And it does not leave the smell of smoke when clearing between clients in your healing practice, clearing your home, and clearing your hotel room when you travel.*

Step 4: Protection

You may be asking - What am I protecting?

Why do I need it?

Your cats and your dogs are most likely more energy sensitive than you are. They're aware of energy that you might not have a clue about. This sensitivity affects their behavior and how they feel.

Your energy field (or energy body, as some people call it) needs an energetic dusting, the same as your physical furniture in your house. This means clearing your energy field of what you have already picked up throughout your day.

Protection can help you and your animals not absorb and not take on energetic clutter around you as you go about your day.

What you are protecting yourself and your animals from is other people's energy, frustrations, anger, and other emotional stuff they are processing and dealing with.

This even goes for people when you are talking on the phone. Animals tune into what is going on. So the disagreement you may have with a family member or friend, your animals pick up on. Or if a friend calls and needs to vent, this is all part of energies coming into your energy field.

Why protections? Just like you put on sunscreen to go out in the sun, you need to put on energetic protections to go into your day. It sets an energetic boundary, so that what is everyone else's is theirs and what is yours is yours. So no matter what you encounter, your energy field stays clean and you feel clear and focused.

A very common way to set up energy protection for yourself is to imagine a white light circling your body about an arm's width out. It goes two feet above your head and two feet below your feet, forming a protective bubble of light around you.

Your protective bubble is semi-permeable. It allows love and good in and out of your energy field, and keeps lower-level energies of others out.

✐ Your Essence Experience ✐

*For extra support, Healing You **Protection** essence is a simple, effective, easy-to-use way to protect yourself from other people's energies and issues. Simply spray the essence three times in the air around you to receive protection support.*

*The **Protection** essence is one you may desire to use daily. When you don't sleep as well or you are not on full energy, **Protection** essence is an easy way to support your energy to stay strong and clear.*

Step 5: Expressing Gratitude

The more gratitude you have, the more things to be grateful for come to you in your life. To keep your vibrations high no matter what is going on in your life, have your first waking thoughts be GOOD MORNING I am so grateful for _____ (whatever that is for you). To support you going throughout your day, I invite you to write down five things you are grateful for in your day. I also invite you to reflect on your gratitude list before going to bed. The more grateful you are for what you have, the more you will receive ease in your life. Giving focus to your gratitude list before you go to sleep will help you be in a better mood, which helps you sleep better.

✑ *Your Essence Experience* ✑

*For extra support, Healing You **Gratitude** essence is a simple, effective, easy-to-use way to share gratitude. Simply spray the essence three times in the air around you to express gratitude to the Universe, opening ways for abundance and prosperity to flow back to you.*

If this feels like a lot of new information to you, it is ok. Becoming aware and being open to this information is a start. This is a process and journey. You have this book to come back to again and again to learn the material at different levels each time you read it. Start with where you are and keep growing at your pace.

Laura, Jillian and Ginger

Laura, along with her miniature labradoodle dog named Ginger, participated in the Animal Connection and Healing Group that this book is modeled after. Ginger was two years old at the time she was participating in the Animal Connection and Healing Group. She had been attacked by a mastiff, had several surgeries with broken bones and lots of stiches when she was younger and had recovered physically. The attack changed Ginger's behavior. Ginger was now always on edge, barking at guests coming to the door, barking and going after the neighbors, even going out into the road after cars. Laura is busy. She works a full-time job, is raising a daughter, and is very active in supporting her daughter's school by coordinating the school auction and more. At the end of this training module in the Animal Connection and Healing Group, Laura's comments were: "I haven't felt this good in a long time." "If this doesn't work for my dog, it will sure work for me." You will hear more about Ginger a little later.

This is why you are here. Helping your precious animal starts with helping yourself.

Homework

For your homework this week, commit to a **time**, commit to a **space** and commit to the **duration** of your session that you will connect with yourself with the intention of grounding, clearing, centering, setting up protection, and expressing gratitude.

Schedule this now on your calendar for this week.

Commit to a minimum of once per week for the next nine weeks for you to have your connection time with your animal. Schedule these on your calendar now for the next nine weeks.

For your first Animal Connection and Healing session, have your animals nearby.

- Ground yourself – Do the grounding cord exercise from Chapter 2.

- Get present – Three deep breaths in and out

- Clear yourself – In the shower and use the Healing You *Clear* essence

- Set up protections – Imagine white light bubble surrounding you

- Express gratitude – Thank the Universe for good in your life

Notice how you feel doing each of these techniques.

Notice what your animal's reaction is to each of these techniques as you are doing them. Notice if your animal seems more interested (perks up, pays attention) during some of these steps more than others.

Notice if your animal is more relaxed, more playful. If you have multiple animals, they may each give you different responses. This is all good information for you going forward with your animal.

In this chapter you learned to prepare you. In the next chapter you will learn how to prepare your environment for conducting an Animal Connection and Healing session with your animal. Let's go...

CHAPTER 3

Preparing Your Environment

THIS CHAPTER IS ABOUT the importance of setting your environment for connecting with your animal. Animals are generally more sensitive than we are. As with people, some animals are more sensitive to energies and environments than others and some are highly sensitive. When their sensitivities are not addressed, behavior issues and physical issues arise.

The main thing is to let go of any expectations or preconceived notions about how your animals will show up. Be open to noticing subtleties, differences that are occurring and remember to have fun.

Healing Activation: Connection

I invite you to step away from whatever you have been doing in your day and allow your attention to be fully in this moment. Be right here, right now. All that has happened and is yet to happen, will be there for you when you get back. Now, take a moment and gently close your eyes. If you are not at a place where you can physically close your eyes, pretend or imagine you can.

Take a moment and check in with how you feel. No judgment, check in and see if there are tight, sore or heavy parts of your body. Check in and see where your body feels good, light, maybe even tingly. Just notice.

I now invite you to take a deep breath in, hold it, let it out. Now take another deep breath in, hold it, let it out. And now for the power of three, take a deep breath in, hold it and let it out. This allows you to become present and be here more fully in the moment.

Now see yourself sitting with your animals and see a new playfulness, a deeper connection, between you and your animals, than you have ever had. There is a sense of deeper understanding, a deeper connection. You can feel it. It feels natural and at the same time almost feels surreal and magical. You have a deeper feeling and awareness than you have had before. There is more connectedness; there is brightness and much more awareness of the energies around you and between you.

With this feeling, see yourself in your favorite place. Your cat/ dog is there with you. There is a smile on your cat's/ dog's face. You see the smile energetically and it is very clear. There is more enthusiasm in your cat/dog connecting with you and you feel very content. You are in awe at the level of clarity and connection you now have between you. Neither of you have to say a word out loud, you both are in connection, contentment and knowing all is well between you. You are wise souls reflecting and contemplating life in appreciation for your time together. All is well.

You can open your eyes.

What we will be covering in this chapter is setting your environment. This is a very important step in setting up your Animal Connection and Healing session with your animal. Setting your environment consists of eight steps.

Setting Your Environment

Step 1: Setting a Time

From Chapter 2 you now have designated time for your Animal Connection and Healing sessions. You marked it on your calendar, so it has

a. Date

b. Time

c. Length of session

This is an important meeting with your animal that your animal does know about and is ready to connect. So make it a time you know you can easily do it.

I recommend allowing 30 minutes for your session – if you have the time and can allocate more time, even better.

In teaching this with the Animal Connection and Healing Group, Joan, a participant, had set the day and time on her calendar for her special connection time with her dog, Briggs. When it came time for their special connection time, Joan was about to do something else. Briggs, however, came to her, reminding Joan by acting in ways she had never seen him act before to ensure he got her attention. She was amazed that Briggs knew. Realizing this, she kept her commitment and time with him. It opened her eyes that Briggs really did know about the meeting and she kept their time sacred to connect together.

As with anything, the more energy you invest in it and the more you practice, the easier and more powerful it will become.

Step 2: Setting the Space

Dedicate a space for your connection times. It can be on the:

   a.   Couch

   b.   Floor

   c.   Rug

   d.   Your bed

   e.   Your cat or dog's bed

   f.   Special relaxation spot

The important thing here is to make it consistent. This will help you while you are learning.

It can be a space that is used for other things as well. For instance, I use my desk to work on my computer for typing my e-zines, doing my bookwork and other business-related tasks. I also sit at my desk when I am doing my distance healing sessions. I set the energies for these scenarios separately for the same physical space. Have it clear in your mind when you are shifting into your Animal Connection and Healing session time with your animal where nothing else is happening at this time.

Step 3: Setting the Environment

This is where you:

    a. Quiet your home phone

    b. Silence your cell phone

    c. Turn your TV off

    d. Turn away from your computer

    e. Turn away from your deadlines and to-do lists

    f. Play soft music

    g. Adjust lighting

The important thing here is, the more comfortable you are, the more comfortable your cat or dog will be and the more comfortable you are the better chance of being clearer where you can connect and communicate.

There can be a tendency to say "oh this step won't matter; I won't take the time to turn off the phone or I will put my cell on vibrate instead of silence" but this is still allowing distractions to come in. Honor your commitment with your animal in making sure all of these steps are in place.

Step 4: Getting Present

Remember from Chapter 2, to take three slow deep breaths in and out one at a time? Taking these breaths will help you leave behind your worries, your to-dos, and allow you to be present and to be clear and ready for your session.

෴ *Your Essence Experience* ෴

*For extra support, Healing You **Iceland Spar** essence is a simple, effective, easy-to-use way to center and get present. Simply spray the essence three times in the air around you to receive centering support. I invite you to take a deep breath in and let it out after spraying the essence. I find this helps it integrate even deeper.*

Step 5: Clearing your space

Jillian with Ginger

Make sure to remove any clutter. Have this be a nice, nurturing, comfortable spot to connect, where both you and your cat/dog are comfortable and feeling special.

෴ *Your Essence Experience* ෴

*For extra support, using Healing Your Animal **Clear** essence is a simple, effective, smokeless, unscented, easy-to-use way to clear your environment. Simply spray the essence three times in the air around your space to receive clearing support.*

Step 6: Stating Your Intentions

This is where you state your intentions for your connection with your animal. Be as clear and specific as possible. For your session this week, you will probably have an intention like this: "My intention is for my cat or dog (fill in your cat or dog's name) and me to have a good connection over the (set duration) next 30 minutes, where we really connect on a different and clearer level. We have a special relationship that will always remain strong. We have a clear channel of communication between us that will grow even stronger each time we connect to communicate."

The important thing is to state your intentions. State what your purpose is so the Universe can provide it to you. And watch for evidence in your session that you were heard and the Universe received your intention. This sets the stage for more clarity and deepening your intentions as you evolve.

Step 7: Having Your Session

The "homework" sections in each chapter describe what to focus on during your session.

The first thing here is to clear your mind and thoughts of any preconceived notions or expectations from your animal and your session. Be open. Be on the lookout and gather any and all information that presents itself to you.

You have two parts to you, an ego and a Spiritual Self. The ego part of you is the doubts, fears and confusion. The Spiritual side of you is love, pure unconditional love where you are connected to your Higher Source, whatever that name is for you: Universe, Spirit, God, Buddha, Source, or Higher Self.

Put your ego self aside and let your Spiritual Self, your Higher Self be present. A technique I like to use is to picture your ego as a basket of puppies. And imagine this basket of puppies outside the space you have set up for your Animal Connection and Healing session with your animal. When thoughts like "am I making this up?" or "did I really get (the information you receive)," "I cannot do this," "oh it's hard," "I'll never be able to do this," "why isn't any information coming to me?" come up, these are the "puppies" to gently put back in the basket, out of your session. This helps you to stay open to what is happening. When a puppy gets out of the basket, gently put the puppy back in the basket and keep connecting with your animal.

Step 8: Closing Your Session

Ask if there is anything else that needs attention before you close. If so, do it.

Step 9: Gratitude

Pet your cat, your dog (or kiss them) and thank them. Let them know you will be connecting with them again. You will know when your next connection time is, since you put it in your calendar.

Jillian and Ginger

Thank the space for supporting you. And now release your space to be used for something else by saying you are finished with this space for your animal connection purpose.

I like taking the extra step and clear the space again to have it clean and ready for its next use. You can spray Healing Your Animal **Clear** essence to clear your environment (space). The benefit of the **Clear** essence is it is a smokeless option and easy to travel with and use anywhere.

If your mind is starting some chatter about how can you do all of this all of the time, no worries. This may seem like a lot, yet it can happen almost instantaneously once you have gotten the hang of it.

Recap

1. Setting Time

    a. Date

    b. Time

    c. Length of session

2. Setting Space

    a. Couch

    b. Floor

    c. Rug

    d. Your bed

    e. Your cat or dog's bed

    f. Special relaxation spot

3. Setting Environment

    a. The more comfortable you are, the more comfortable your cat and dog will be

4. Getting Present

    a. Three slow, deep breaths

    b. Extra support: Healing Your Animal *Iceland Spar* essence

5. Clearing Your Space

    a. Clear the area from any clutter

    b. Have your space be nurturing and comfortable

    c. It is important for you and your animal to feel comfortable and special. This is a special connection time for you

     d. Extra support: Healing Your Animal *Clear* essence

6. Stating Your Intentions

7. Having Your Session

8. Closing Your Session

9. Gratitude

     a. Extra support: Healing Your Animal **Gratitude** essence

10. Clear Your Space When You Are Finished

     a. Extra support: Healing Your Animal *Clear* essence

Homework

This week for your Connection and Healing Time:

1. Prepare You – Grounding, Getting Present, Clearing, and Protection from Chapter 2.

2. Set your environment with the steps from this chapter.

3. Sit with your animal and tell him or her all that you love about your time together and all that you appreciate him or her.

4. Share your funniest memories of how he or she has made you laugh. You can even sit with a photo album if you have one of your animal and go through it from the beginning when they came into your life through now. The feelings that are evoked in you will be conveyed and felt by your animal companion in a big way.

5. Pay attention to your animal's actions, reactions and responses during this time. Notice all of the subtleties, body language, energy level, attention and focus. Are they more playful, or going to their food bowl? Whatever it is they are doing, pay attention to what you were saying and feeling at the time of their actions. This will give you a lot of information. It might not make sense at first. No worries, we are here to put it together and get clarity.

6. Journal it, so you can track if it happens again with the same corresponding thoughts and feelings. This will start giving you more insight and help you "listen" to your animals in a different way.

7. Close your session by thanking your animal for this time together.

Celebrate! This step is bigger than just this session. It is a foundational step that will support you going forward.

Post your experience with your session on the Healing You, Healing Your Animal Facebook group.

In this chapter, you learned to prepare your environment. In the next chapter you will learn how to prepare your animal for receiving a healing session. Ready? Let's go...

CHAPTER 4

Preparing Your Animal

YOUR ANIMALS LOVE YOU so much that they take on your "stuff" to help you, whether you ask them to or not. In Chapter 2, you heard my story and how Tasha taught me about clearing the stuff she was taking on and was not able to clear on her own.

Opening, balancing and clearing your animal's chakras and your own is a great way to support you and your animals with optimum health, calming and boosting confidence. For those of you not familiar with chakras, they are energy centers in your body and in your animal's body.

No worries if this is new to you, I will guide and support you, so stay open and allow the process to support you. Your animals understand this and love receiving this.

The main thing is to let go of any expectations or preconceived notions in how your animals will show up. Be open to noticing subtleties and differences that are occurring, and remember to have fun.

The intention of this Healing Activation is to support you with getting familiar and in touch with your chakras. As you are getting in touch with your chakras, there is a healing shift occurring for you and your animals. Your chakras and your animals' are being cleared and balanced. This Healing Activation helps to open chakras where they may be blocked or not fully open and brings chakras that are too open into balance for harmonious flow, promoting optimum health.

As I am educating you where your chakras are, I invite you to place your hands on each chakra while clearing and balancing them. Your animals are healing (clearing and balancing their chakras too) as we are going through this. The purpose is clearing and balancing your chakras together, which helps you get more aligned and more connected with your animals. If you have multiple animals, this is happening simultaneously. Energy is not linear. You don't have to do it for one person, then one animal, then your next animal, etc. It can all happen at the same time.

I am sensitive to energy when shifts are happening. I may yawn, take a deep breath, or cough. All of these are signs that energy is shifting and moving. You may or may not notice the shifts in this way; everyone is different.

As we go through this, you will notice the chakras follow the colors of the rainbow.

Healing Activation: Balancing Chakras

I invite you to step away from whatever you have been doing in your day and allow your attention to be fully in this moment. Be right here, right now. All that has happened and yet to happen, will be there for you when you get back. Now, take a moment and gently close your eyes. If you are not at a place where you can physically close your eyes, pretend or imagine you can.

Take a moment and check in with how you feel. No judgment, check in and see if there are tight, sore or heavy parts of your body. Check in and see where your body feels good, light, maybe even tingly. Just notice.

I now invite you to take a deep breath in, hold it, let it out. Now take another deep breath in, hold it, let it out. And now for the power of three, take a deep breath in, hold it and let it out. This allows you to become present and more fully in the moment.

As we are starting our way on this journey:

Chakra 1 is the Root Chakra. It is located at the base of your spine, its color is red, and it is closest to the earth with the densest frequency. It represents survival and safety.

Place your hands on your lower pelvic region. Imagine your root chakra is cleansing and clearing all that is no longer needed and allowing in the energy of a balanced healthy root chakra.

Chakra 2 is the Sacral Chakra. It is located two inches below your navel, its color is orange. This chakra represents your sexuality, your creativity, the birthing not only of a physical child, it is birthing of new ideas and projects, the center of your creativity and passions.

Place your hands on your lower abdomen two inches below your navel. Imagine your sacral chakra is cleansing and clearing all that is no longer needed and allowing in the energy of a balanced healthy sacral chakra.

Chakra 3 is the Solar Plexus Chakra. It is located between your belly button and the base of your rib cage, its color is yellow, it is your center of power, center of will, it is how you present yourself to the world. It is also your center of manifestation, when you state your desires and intentions into the world, they can be answered and delivered to you.

Place your hands on your abdomen above your navel and below your rib cage. Imagine your solar plexus chakra is cleansing and clearing all that is no longer needed and allowing in the energy of a balanced healthy solar plexus chakra.

Chakra 4 is the Heart Chakra. It is located in the center of your chest, its color is green, the center of love, unconditional love, and compassion. This is the connection with oneness with everyone. From your heart, this chakra represents a universal language of love; this goes for your animals too. They know and sense this love and connect on the heart level.

Place your hands on your chest. Imagine your heart chakra is cleansing and clearing all that is no longer needed and allowing in the energy of a balanced, healthy heart chakra.

Chakra 5 is the Throat Chakra. It is located in the center of your throat, its color is sky blue. It is the center for speaking your truth, clarity of speaking, your voice, and expressing your true self. You are speaking your truth, your dogs are barking, your cats are meowing – for purity of speech.

Place your hands on your throat. Imagine your throat chakra is cleansing and clearing all that is no longer needed and allowing in the energy of a balanced healthy throat chakra.

Chakra 6 is the Third Eye Chakra. It is located in the center of your forehead, its color is indigo blue. This is your center of intuition, your clarity, this is 360-degree vision. As humans, a lot of the time we are "in our head." You may have heard the saying, "shift from your head to your heart" or "get grounded." As this chakra opens, it brings the energies from all of the mental activity down into your heart center and your root chakra, opening your being to be connected with the present moment here on the Earth.

Place your hands on your forehead. Imagine your third eye chakra is cleansing and clearing all that is no longer needed and allowing in the energy of a balanced, healthy third eye chakra.

Chakra 7 is the Crown Chakra. It is located on the top of your head, its color is light purple or white with gold. This is your connection center to God, Source, Higher Power, Universe, whatever that term is to you. When this chakra is open, you get crystal clear connection here, guidance and support.

Place your hands on the top of your head. Imagine your crown chakra is cleansing and clearing all that is no longer needed and allowing in the energy of a balanced, healthy crown chakra.

You and your animals now have your chakras a little more open and balanced than when we started. Doing this together with your animal helps you get in sync with one another, deepens connection and enhances communication on multiple levels.

Check in and notice how you feel. Has there been a change in your body from when we started? Notice what those changes are.

You can open your eyes.

Do you have animals who are what you might call "helter skelter," who are all over the place, scattered? They are not focused. They are distracted by lots of things. For cats, they may be running around getting into mischief with high speed. I call this the "zoomies." For dogs, they may be barking a lot and you have no idea why. They are pacing, being busy bodies. I equate it to children who cannot sit still. It is the same with your cats and your dogs. For your cats and dogs who cannot sit still, cannot focus, are scattered and all over the place, grounding would be highly beneficial.

Pablo is a cat who needs a lot of grounding support. When he is not grounded, he runs all over the place and you cannot get his focus. He attacks his "brother" Vincent and runs wild around the house until he tires himself out. Now that Sally knows about grounding for herself and Pablo, Pablo has a lot fewer episodes of running sporadically around the house. And Sally knows to check in with her energy when Pablo is running wild. She has seen the correlation with Pablo being affected and more active when she hasn't grounded herself.

Sally and Pablo

Grounding takes place in the root chakra, chakra 1. Your root chakra is about survival – safety, food, water, and shelter.

Safety

It is important that your cat/dog has a safe spot that is there to retreat to when they choose to be alone. It is a dedicated place for your cat/dog. It is a fun, safe place.

For cats, have a place where they can get up high. They like heights. If you have an older cat, make sure you have a place to retreat to that is clearly theirs – a cube fleece bed is one option. For dogs, you can have a crate with the door open.

Have a bed for them in the living room and bedroom (if you allow them in the bedroom).

Food

It is important to feed your animals good-quality food. How do you know if it is good quality food? Buy your food at the animal health stores. They specialize in carrying good quality food, making sure the ingredients are from a good source.

I had a client, Bear, a German shepherd who was barely able to walk and on Rimadyl, which is a hard-core pain killer. Bear was switched to a raw diet and within a week, he was noticeably moving better, having more energy. This made an impact on me to see how significant Bear's change was in one week. I realized just how important food is for our body and quality of health. In a short time with his new diet and massages, Bear was walking so much better, feeling so much better, and off the hard-core pain killer. He was a totally different dog.

Australian veterinarian Ian Billinghurst brought forth the idea of feeding raw food to pets in 1993 in his book "Give Your Dog a Bone." He called his feeding the BARF diet

(Bones and Raw Food, or Biologically Appropriate Raw Food). Since this book came out, other raw food diets have emerged that include some frozen and freeze-dried options. If choosing raw, please research and do what resonates with you. Also make sure you provide your animals with the proper balance of ingredients that supports your animal's optimum health.

An important thing to know is that cats and dogs have different dietary needs, so do not feed them the same food. Get educated before starting a raw diet.

Feeding raw is a personal choice. It is not for everyone. And it doesn't always fit your lifestyle.

My point here is sharing that the quality of food you feed your cat/dog does matter.

With the clients who feed their cats/dogs good-quality food, I have seen a difference in the quality of their cat's/dog's muscles, their coat and overall health.

Veterinarians are not trained in nutritional care for the animals in regular vet school. The vets who are up on the best foods for your cat/dog have taken extra training. It is a myth that the foods vets carry in their clinic are the best quality of food for your animal. I know first-hand. I fed my cats a diet recommended by my vet for years thinking I was feeding them good food. It came from the vet, it cost more; therefore, it must be good for them. Boy was I wrong. It was filled with fillers and what we would equate to "junk" food.

A good general rule of thumb is get your food for your cat/dog at an animal health food store.

Here is an important piece of information for you to be aware of. Your animals can have sensitivities and allergies to food just like we do. So if your cat/dog is itching a lot, licking a lot, having gas, red bumps, sores on the stomach, or diarrhea, this may be an indication to switch foods.

This is something I support my private clients with. Determining if your animal's body is going to accept the food, absorb it and be able to process it in a supportive way or if it is constricting and having a reaction in some way. If there is an issue, we hone in on what ingredient your cat/dog is reacting to.

Food preparation: It is important for you to pay attention to the mood you are in as you are preparing your cat's or dog's food. If you are angry and grumpy putting your animal's food together, your angry grumpy energy goes into the food. And then you serve it where your cat/dog eats this food. Even if you aren't angry with your cat/dog, your anger energy goes into the food you just prepared and served and then your precious cat/dog takes in your anger when eating this food.

I invite you to be conscious and add loving energies to your animal's food as you are preparing it and putting it down, serving it to him/her. Then they have this loving energy feeding them and nourishing them as they eat their food.

This is something to be mindful of when preparing your food too.

Routine

Your animals like routine.

Walking 20 minutes a day in the fresh air supports strengthening your immune system and it is grounding.

For cats:

Some people put harnesses on their cats and take walks; however, not all cats will walk on a leash. So take your walk whether with or without your cat.

The best way to support your cat is to engage your cat in active play where his/her hunting instincts get activated. For instance, place a feather on a string and connect it to a pole/wand and move it around. Have your cat jump and chase the feather. This releases the cortisol in your cat's fight or flight mechanism, boosting his/her immune system.

For dogs:

A regular walk is good for you and your dog.

Some of you may have heard to walk your dog for what your dog needs, what is best for him, to his/her level, etc. How do you know what his or her level is?

Start with a 20-minute walk. You can start at a slower pace and build up your pace. Take notice, is your dog having trouble keeping up? Is your dog really winded? Is your dog still full of pep at the end? These are things to gauge if a longer walk or faster-paced walk would benefit your dog.

Animals who have been rescued really benefit from grounding.

Kathy first started working with me when Samson her 10-year-old Cocker Spaniel fell off the bed one morning and couldn't walk. She had taken Samson to the vet and he had also received acupuncture with not much improvement. Kathy wasn't sure how it was going to work with me being near Seattle and Samson being in Calgary, Alberta Canada. She decided to see. She previously had to hold up Samson to go potty because he could not stand on his own. Within five minutes after his first session, she took him out and he was able to stand and pee on his own. This was such a great relief for Kathy and Brent, her partner. Samson continued to full recovery.

After Samson passed, Kathy rescued Beamer, a 10-year-old Bichon Frise. He was nervous and skittish around people, including Kathy and Brent at first. He had trust issues; most rescued animals have this in common. When doing the Animal Connection and Healing Group, Beamer really loved the grounding techniques and support and blossomed during this group. He is much more comfortable in his daily life. His walks are much easier. Kathy sent in a picture of Beamer joyfully sitting in her neighbor's lap. He's now started to actually go up to people in the park and when they hold out their hand for him to sniff - he does! This is a huge change for him from where he started. It turns out he loves other dogs. He is great with them. He met his first cat and decided he likes cats, too. With Kathy and Beamer working with me privately, Beamer continues to blossom every day and Kathy continues to use the techniques in this book.

Preparing Your Animal for Your Session

Step 1: Grounding Your Animal

Believe it or not, animals need grounding too. Just like people, some animals are naturally more grounded than others. Anxious animals will highly benefit from grounding. Grounding works for cats, dogs, horses and other animals too.

One Animal Connection and Healing Group participant, Mary Kay, was extremely worried about her dog, Kizzi. Kizzi would bolt out the door when it opened and run into the road. She had previously been hit by a car twice. Mary Kay was stressed, wondering if the next bolt would be Kizzi's last. By participating in the Animal Connection and Healing Group and using these techniques, Kizzi had a tremendous shift. She was more relaxed. She stopped bolting out the door. She was very comfortable in her home. Mary Kay was more relaxed and life was more enjoyable. A later report is that Kizzi still has not bolted out the door since this shift in the group. Awesome news.

Here is a great way to ground your animal:

Place your hands on top of your animal's paw as it is on the floor. Imagine sending energy down through your hand through your animal's paw and deep into the earth below the floor. This supports connecting your animal's paws to the ground to help them feel the grounding effect.

Start with the front paws.

Vicki grounding X's front paws

When you are grounding an animal that is unsettled and hyper, place one hand on the collar to support settling the animal as you are grounding with the other hand, as shown in this photo.

Now for the back paws.

Vicki grounding X's back paws

As with the grounding the front paws, you may need to keep one hand on the collar while you shift to ground the back paws.

Sometimes when grounding, you may feel your animal trying to bring his paw back up and not stay down to the ground. When your animal needs grounding, it feels funny and different to him/her to be grounding. Be patient while your animal is getting used to this new feeling and way of being.

It would serve your animal to have regular daily grounding support.

As you can see in this photo, X is getting more relaxed and grounded, and now two hands are being used on the front paws to facilitate grounding.

Vicki using the two-handed grounding technique with X

Now X is totally relaxed, fully grounded.

X is fully grounded

Note: This series of photos shows the full range of possibilities for grounding a dog. Not all cats or dogs will get to this fully relaxed stage when you first introduce them to grounding. Be happy with the level your animal attains.

✌ Your Essence Experience ✌

For extra support, Healing Your Animal **Ground** *essence is a simple, effective, easy-to-use way to ground your animal. Simply spray the essence three times in the air around you to receive grounding support.*

Step 2: Clearing Your Animal

In Chapter 2, Tasha showed us how important it is to clear for both you and your animal.

Here is a story about Wendy and her cat, Moonbeam.

Moonbeam was very sensitive to energy. And some of Moonbeam's behaviors when energy needed to be cleared in her environment (including Wendy, her guardian) were hiding behind the refrigerator, not sleeping with Wendy, and pooping outside the litter box.

Wendy had tried everything, taking Moonbeam to the vet, acupuncture, reiki, working with multiple powerful healers, but Moonbeam's issues kept coming back until Wendy started clearing. Wendy was very resistant to clearing. She couldn't feel any of what Moonbeam was feeling, so she didn't really see the need for the extra care and attention that Moonbeam was needing. Because of not being able to see, feel or experience this, Wendy was truly resistant. After great lengths and conversations with Moonbeam and Wendy, Wendy regularly took the steps to clear and saw the difference in Moonbeam.

Moonbeam had a clear message for Wendy, and when Wendy started to take heart and take action, Moonbeam started doing better. This opening and clearly visible results that Moonbeam was doing better warmed Wendy's heart, and helped Wendy realize her extra efforts were worth it. This helped Wendy relieve her stress and worry. She felt immensely better and was motivated to keep clearing to help Moonbeam.

Wendy recognized that Moonbeam was helping her raise her consciousness. And she thanks me with great heart-warming gratitude for helping her get Moonbeam to feeling much more playful, have more bonding and connection and a better quality of life in general while being together.

The stories of Tasha and Moonbeam help show that all of the stressors you have and encounter are then transferred to your loving cat or dog. You come home feeling tired, feeling like you have dealt with enough stress in your day, you greet your cat/dog and you pet them. You immediately feel better because your animal has just helped you clear your stresses from you. Now, they are carrying your energy around and need to get it cleared.

And no matter how much you tell your animal not to take on your stuff, they love you so much they will anyway.

So you can support your animal by clearing them.

Here is a clearing technique I call "tip of nose to tip of tail" for clearing your animal.

Put on an imaginary energy protection glove – similar to putting on a glove to wash your dishes. Set your intention that it will protect you from taking on your animal's energy that you are clearing.

Hold your hand two to four inches above your animal's body. Start with your hand over the nose and run your hand above your animal's body, down the center line all the way to the base of his/her tail. As you are doing this, envision collecting everything that is no longer needed from your animal's energy field into your hand as you make your pass from the nose, over the forehead, down the back of the head, over the shoulders, down the center of the back, over the hips, out the base of the tail.

Vicki clearing X, starting at the head

Vicki clearing X, ending with the tail and flicking off energy

Once you have completed this, imagine you are flicking the energy off into an energy recycle bin to remove it from your hand, with your glove still on. Once you have discarded the collected energy, you can take off your energy protection glove. The intention is to let go of all of the energy that is no longer needed, what is ready to release, what isn't your animal's energy that he/she collected throughout the day. The intention is that his/her energy field is replenished with light, optimal health and healing, and vibrant energies.

You can also use two hands to do this clearing technique.

Vicki using the two-hand clearing technique with X

✍ Your Essence Experience ✍

*For extra support, Healing Your Animal **Clear** essence is a simple, effective, easy-to-use way to clear your animal's energy field. Simply spray the essence three times in the air around your animal to receive clearing support.*

Step 3: Protections for Your Animal

Why protections? Just like you learned in Chapter 2, you put on sunscreen to go out in the sun, and you need to put on energetic protections to go into your day. It sets an energetic boundary that what is others is theirs and what is yours is yours.

This works the same with your animals.

Your animal takes on your stuff whether you want him/her to or not. And think about how many people your animal is around during the day. And as people reach down to give him/her a pet, your animal may take on others' issues as well.

I recommend that you provide protection so that no matter what your animal encounters, your animal stays clean, clear and focused.

The same white bubble of light you put around yourself, you are going to put around your animal. Here is the protection technique we learned in Chapter 2:

A very common way to set up energy protection for yourself is to imagine a white light circling your body about an arm's width out. It goes two feet above your head and two feet below your feet, forming a protective bubble of light around you.

Vicki forming a protective bubble around X

Your protective bubble is semi-permeable. It allows love and good in and out of your energy field, and keeps lower-level energies of others out.

I find that animals who are feeling insecure, unsafe, submissive and shy really like the energetic protections. It helps them feel safe, so they become more confident and engaging.

Lucy, a rat terrier, is very skittish by nature. She competed in agility, obedience and rally obedience. I went to see her compete and grounded her and set up protection for her before going into the ring. Sue, Lucy's guardian, and other spectators familiar with Lucy commented that was the calmest and most focused they had seen her in the ring and wanted to know what I did.

Lucy was my very first agility dog to support so she holds a special place in my heart for opening that door to all of the many agility dogs I have been blessed to support in performing their best and having fun.

Setting up protections is especially important when your animal is sick. Your animal needs all of his/her energy to focus on healing, so keeping out what isn't your animal's energy helps your animal stay stronger. This is true whether your animal is going to rebound and recover or it is his/her time to transition.

It is also important for all animals in the household to have energy protections especially when one animal is sick.

Just as animals take on our stuff to help us clear, animals can take on other animals' stuff to help them.

As a responsible dog guardian, Sheri had been working with me for wellness and connecting deeper with her two Whippet dogs, Niko and Levi, along with her traditional vet for holistic care.

Niko got diagnosed with hemangiosarcoma with mast cells. It was too far along for treatment.

You heard me mention Tasha was my "heart" cat in the dedication. Niko was Sheri's "heart" dog and he was her first dog. Emotions were high. Sheri was grounding, clearing and protecting herself, Niko, and Levi to support all of them as they navigated through Niko's transitioning.

It was important to include and keep Levi grounded, cleared and protected and honoring him too during this process, since most of the attention was going to Niko to support him feeling his best and having a good quality of life during this time.

Levi is Sheri's "play" dog. Levi's way of helping Sheri was by being playful. It was important for Sheri to acknowledge Levi for his playfulness even when she was sad. This helped ease her mind knowing how Levi was connecting with her through this process.

"Wrapping up with Niko would have been so much harder if we had not been working with Vicki before all of that began. I would have felt like I was floundering without Vicki's support. I did not know what was available and with Vicki it just becomes a way that you relate to your pack and it isn't complicated. I feel like I got as good a deal helping that dog go home as was possible to get and I would have always wondered if Vicki hadn't been there. To feel like I got to hear from him just makes all of the difference. That he was not suffering, he did not feel good and he was tired and he was done. I knew where he stood and that helped me know where I was supposed to stand."

Sheri Mortko, Olathe, KS

ꙮ *Your Essence Experience* ꙮ

If you find your animal is still insecure, submissive and shy, for extra protection, I invite you to use Healing Your Animal **Protection** *Essence.*

If your animal is sick, I highly recommend using Healing Your Animal **Protection** *Essence.*

It is a simple, effective, easy-to-use way to protect you and your animal. Simply spray the essence three times in the air around you and your animal to receive protection support.

If you recall from Chapter 2, the **Protection** *essence is one you may desire to use daily. When you don't sleep well or do not have your full energy,* **Protection** *essence is an easy way to support your energy and an easy way to support your animal's energy to stay strong.*

Step 4 Gratitude

Express gratitude to your animal for your connection. Express gratitude for the space providing this connection. Feel the love and connection between you and your animal. Ask if there is anything else your animal needs before completing your connection. If there is something your animal needs, do that. Then close with gratitude until your next connection.

⁂ *Your Essence Experience* ⁂

*For extra support, Healing Your Animal **Gratitude** essence is a simple, effective, easy-to-use way to express gratitude to your animal. Simply spray the essence three times in the air around you to send gratitude out to the Universe, opening the flow for your prosperity and your animal's. (From your animal's perspective, prosperity means more love, hugs, rubs, treats, toys.)*

Kim, Biscuit and Brulee

Kim first came to me when she got her puppies, Biscuit and Brulee. She was asking for support with potty training. When I got to her home and connected with Biscuit and Brulee, I discovered that Brulee really was not feeling well. Kim had already taken them both to the vet and the vet said Biscuit and Brulee were healthy. From my assessment, Brulee was very depleted energetically. She welcomed and received the healing energy. She felt better at the end of the session; however, she was not out of the woods from my assessment. She was running around being a puppy, so Kim did not know the extent of how bad she was feeling.

When I work with people and their animals, I take my role seriously and I treat each animal with the same love and care as if they are my own. I noticed Biscuit was a little off; yet he was much stronger than Brulee so it was unclear if he was feeling that way by helping Brulee clear her issue (as animals do for each other as well as for their guardians) or if he had a slight case too. Following up with Kim, she was open to me coming back to check out Biscuit and Brulee. I couldn't shake the feeling that something was really off even though the vet had not found anything. Brulee was somewhat stronger; yet depleted again energetically. She responded to her session and I insisted Kim take Brulee back to the vet and request some tests. The results showed Biscuit and Brulee both had giardia and it was really taking a toll on Brulee.

Kim decided to take my Animal Connection and Healing Group program to help Biscuit and Brulee with understanding them better, taking good care of them and learning healing techniques she could do to support them live happy and healthy lives.

Brulee and Biscuit

Remember in the beginning when I said anything is possible? During the Animal Connection and Healing Group after doing the chakra balancing activation, Kim's life really opened up. Her business took off and kept evolving. She received a big promotion. She has a new serious love relationship in her life. She is really flourishing.

Kim and the whole family

The techniques here are really for the whole of your and your animal's lives.

Homework

Use your dedicated session connection time and location to connect with your animal for the intention of healing and grounding, clearing and protecting your animal this week.

For cat guardians – do the playing exercises discussed in this chapter where your cat is jumping, chasing, and running after the toy on the end of the pole/line.

For dog guardians – dogs need daily exercise. And putting them in the backyard isn't enough. Do a 20-minute focused walk daily with your dog at a minimum. You will benefit from exercising together and receive the extra benefit of bonding by being together.

In Your Connection and Healing Session:

1. Prepare yourself with grounding, getting present, clearing and protecting that you learned from Chapter 2.

2. Take your time with each technique and notice your response when you ground, clear and protect yourself. Also notice your animal's response to you as you ground, clear and protect.

3. Prepare your environment with the steps from Chapter 3.

4. Prepare your animal with grounding, clearing, and protecting that you learned in this chapter.

5. Notice your animal's responses when you ground, clear and protect him/her.

6. What techniques did your animal respond to best? What response or behavior did your animal have? A special look or action or something else?

7. Were the techniques you responded to the most the same ones or different ones that your animal responded to the most?

8. Post your session experience on the Healing You, Healing Your Animal Facebook group.

Celebrate! This is another foundational step that will support you with having a loving, healing bond with your animal.

In this chapter you learned to prepare your animal for an Animal Connection and Healing session with the energy techniques of grounding, clearing and protecting. In the next chapter you will learn calming techniques. This will help calm you and your animals. So if your cat or dog has not been willing to sit still with you, this will help. Let's go...

CHAPTER 5

Calming Techniques

MY INTENTION IS TO PROVIDE a very powerful calming chapter so that you gain calming skills in helping you deepen your connection and calming for you and your animals.

Healing Activation: Calming

Take a moment and close your eyes. If you are not at a place where you can close your eyes, pretend or imagine you can. As you are closing your eyes, I invite you to come and be present to here and now. Whatever has already been happening in your day can be put aside. It can wait outside the door, and it and whatever else needs your attention will be there when you are finished with this chapter. This is a gift you are giving yourself. Not only for yourself, for your animals as well.

Now I invite you to take a deep breath in, hold it, let it out. As your breath is cleansing and clearing, paving the way for you to relax, be more in this moment. Let's take another deep breath in, hold it, let it out. As you are relaxing, letting go, and being here more fully, let's take another deep breath in, hold it and let it go.

As you return to normal breathing, feel your breaths swirling through your physical body and integrating; notice how your body feels. Is it more open, are you able to breathe in more fully, more deeply? Just notice, no judgment. As you are paying attention to your breaths, imagine you are walking on the beach on a nice warm sunny day, a light breeze is blowing and the temperature is just perfect for you to relax, be open, enjoy seeing and hearing the waves of the ocean. And as you are walking, you are noticing how easy it is to walk. You are free, your hair is blowing in the wind and you don't have any cares, you are feeling joyful and content. You have a calming presence that is coming all the way from deep inside you. Maybe you notice people flying kites on the beach, children playing further down the beach, and you are content walking, being with yourself, being with Source. You notice seagulls gracefully flying. And imagine yourself flying alongside them, being carried by the current of the wind, light and free with the wind in your hair. As you glide gracefully through the air, you notice how light you are as you are supported. It is natural to feel free.

Now imagine yourself gliding down to the ocean and landing on a gentle wave. It feels fun as you float and are moving with the wave. See yourself floating in the ocean not far from the beach. You are weightless and supported by the awesome ocean. As you are floating you are calm. You are being carried by the ocean, closer and closer to the beach. You are feeling this calm all through your body. Now as you are floating on a gentle wave, this wave takes you back to shore, back to the beach, where you carefully stand up and continue walking, reflecting and embracing how calm, free and open you feel.

Your animals are there on the beach, happy to greet you. This beach is a special beach just for you and your animals. You open your arms wide and give them a big hug and laugh as they are happy to see you. There is a deeper connection when you connect at this time. They feel the calmness of your experience, they are open and calm and happy that you are much more available to them at this moment. You spread a blanket and lie together on the beach calmly, connected and bonding, totally content, in harmony and understanding each other very clearly. You each have a warm, glowing, togetherness smile on your faces. Take a moment to feel this and embrace this.

You can open your eyes.

The calmer you are, the calmer your animal will be. And there is a reciprocal thing happening between you and your animal.

Did you know by petting your cat, your dog, you are lowering your blood pressure? This is a medical fact. Petting your animal lowers your blood pressure, so they are helping you calm. And the calmer you are, the calmer your animals will be, so you are helping each other at the same time.

Signs of Release and Response

There are signs and things to pay attention to and notice to give you information that your animal is truly responding to what you are doing with the calming techniques.

Pay Attention

Some of the effects of doing the calming techniques that you will learn in this chapter will be obvious:

- Relaxed stretch
- Deep sigh
- Yawn
- Appreciative look
- Eyes softening
- Clear drainage from nose

Others, such as the following are more subtle and may go unnoticed unless you are paying attention.

- Tiny muscle spasms
- Minute shifts in alignment
- Easing of tension in a muscle or muscle group
- A change in breathing pattern

Benefit

Still others are likely to register first subconsciously:

- The deepening bond between you and your animal
- The improvement in technique
- The way your animal begins to direct the session (sits or lies down, presents his/her body part that would like attention first)

Finally, there are the effects that using the healing techniques with your animal have on you: a lowering of blood pressure and stress level and a greater appreciation for your animal as an individual with his/her own personality, likes and dislikes.

Calming Techniques

Take a Deep Breath

Animals are sensitive to their environment.

By taking a deep breath, you are calming yourself, which calms your animal.

I encourage you to take three deep breaths in and out, one at a time, as you did in the healing activations.

Two Hands on Animal

Placing two hands on your animal provides a closed circuit of energy that is calming to your animal.

Vicki using two hand connection to calm X

You can try this for yourself. Place one hand on your leg and have your other hand in the air. Check in and see how you feel. Now place the hand that is in the air down on your other leg so that you now have both hands connecting to your legs. Check in and see how you feel. Can you sense the difference? Your animals sure can.

When working with your animal, always use the two-hand connection. The photo below shows one hand working and the other hand resting on the dog's body. (When one hand is working a specific spot, it doesn't matter where the second hand rests as long as there is a connection with the animal's body.)

Vicki using another two-hand technique to calm X

Talk in a Low, Soothing Voice

We have talked about the fact that the calmer you are, the calmer your animal will be.

The reverse is also true. Have you ever noticed when you are excited, your animals are excited?

When you speak in a high-pitched, fast voice, your animals will be excited.

Talking in a low, soothing, slow voice is very comforting and calming to your animal.

The calmer, slower, and lower your tone of voice, the more calming it is for your animal. This really soothes animals that are very frightened and helps them relax.

Three-Point Acupressure Calming Hold

The acupressure points called GB 20 are located at the base of the skull a little distance away from the center of the head. You will feel little arches in the base of the skull and your fingers will fit lightly in the dip of the arch on both sides of the skull.

The acupressure point GV 20 is located in the center of the top of the head in a little dip. It is located in front of the external protuberance (bump on the head).

Engaging both of the GB 20 acupressure points together is calming.

Adding in the GV 20 at the same time adds to the calming effect with your animals.

With one hand, place your thumb and middle finger on each of the GB 20 acupressure points with a light touch. Place your index finger on the GV 20 acupressure point. Place your other hand somewhere on your animal's body for a two-hand connection.

Vicki using three-point acupressure calming with X

TIP: If your dog is a bigger breed and your hand is not big enough to reach all three points with one hand, here is how you can engage the points. With one hand, place your thumb on one of the GB 20 acupressure points and either your middle finger or your ring finger on the other GB 20 acupressure point. With your other hand, place your middle finger on the GV 20 on the top of the head.

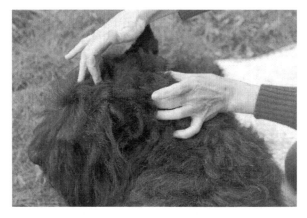

Vicki using two-hand acupressure calming with X

Third eye — Between Eyebrows

The center of the forehead in the chakra system is Chakra 6, also called the third eye, or the brow, and in acupressure it is called the Yin Tang point. This is a very calming point when touched. Lightly rub your index or middle finger up the bridge of your animal's nose to the center of his/her forehead. Continue rubbing up the bridge of the nose for more calming.

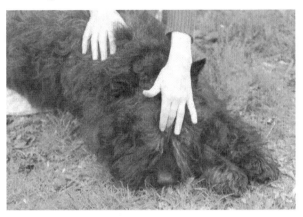

Vicki using third eye calming technique with X

CV17 — Center of chest

The acupressure point CV17 stands for Central Vessel 17, also called Conception Vessel 17, and it is located in the center of the chest.

I like to teach you on yourself, so you can then understand and translate that to your animal easily. (And you benefit yourself.)

It is located in the center of the breast bone (sternum) on the line of your nipples at birth. (As we age, nipples may sag, it's a fact of life.) The point is, the correct point is along the line of where your nipples were at birth in the center of your chest.

Locate the center of your breast bone. Usually there is a small hollow in the breast bone (sternum) where your finger can rest to engage CV17. Hold this point for a minute. If unsure where the point is, gently hold your hand on your breast bone for a minute to receive the benefit of calming.

Now, place your whole hand on the center of your animal's chest. You are engaging the CV17 acupressure point along with your hand connecting to the heart chakra. This is the passive touch massage stroke when you place your hand on the body gently and hold. It is very calming to your animal for your hand to be placed on his/her chest. Remember the two-hand connection? Lightly place your other hand somewhere on your animal's body.

Vicki calming X with two-hand connection

Rubbing Ears

Your ears and your animal's ears contain many acupressure points that correspond with your whole body. Stimulating the acupressure points in the ears increases flow and boosts your organs' functioning in a healthy way. It increases the quality of life for you and your animals. It is very calming for you as well as for your animals.

Vicki rubbing X's ears

Grounding Hold on Sacrum (Low Back)

This is especially great for fearful animals.

Lightly place your whole hand on the low back of your animal. This light touch that is stationary is called the passive touch massage stroke. It is the only massage stroke that is safe to do across the spine. You will have part of your hand on top of one hip, one part of your hand across the low back and one part of your hand on top of the other hip. This is a very gentle placement of your hand on your animal's low back. Your hand lightly rests on your animal's low back.

This is very grounding and provides a calming. This is especially good to support fearful animals to feel safer and begin to relax.

Remember to use two-hand connection.

Vicki using two-hand connection calming with X

To increase the calming benefits, place your other hand gently on your animal's chest. (Note: a nervous or excited dog will be standing or sitting up where you can easily reach the chest.)

In Chapter 4 you heard about Mary Kay and Kizzi. Mary Kay also has a dog, Camo, who would growl at guests, get overexcited and nip at them. Here is what Mary Kay had to say:

"My favorite part about this (Animal Connection and Healing) group is that I've noticed that both of my dogs seem to be calmer. Kizzi is not driven to run away anymore. And she seems to be much more content with her home here. Camo seems to be more secure in his position. He doesn't feel he has to be as protective and dominant over people who come to visit. Previously he would get excited over every move someone made when they came to visit; now he is calmer. Camo used to overeat. Every time he walked by the food bowl he would eat

and was gaining some weight. He doesn't do that anymore. So he is healthier."

Mary Kay Grossman, Spokane, WA

Another client, Jocelyn, has this to say about the changes that her dog and her family have made:

"Sanjah Anna, our 4-year-old German Shepherd, is excessively ecstatic in the way she greets company (jumping, barking, and urinating). Vicki experienced this behavior when she came to do a session with our older Shepherd, Nike. Vicki brought the **Serene** *essence on her next visit and after coming in the door sprayed near Sanjah. Within SECONDS Sanjah calmed down! My mouth dropped open. We've been using* **Serene** *ever since for Sanjah when the doorbell rings. This opened our eyes and we are now using the essences ourselves."*

Jocelyn Paluch, Spokane, WA

⨖ Your Essence Experience ⨖

Healing Your Animal **Serene** *essence is a simple, effective, easy-to-use way to calm anxiety.*

Healing Your Animal **Separation Ease** *essence is a calming formula created for cats and dogs with separation anxiety, where they get nervous when they are separated from their guardians.*

Simply spray the essence three times in the air around you to receive calming support.

"*I was introduced to Vicki through my sister since I like to use alternative medications whenever possible. Up until literally December of 2015, I have used other sprays along with my lavender essential oils to help calm the companion animals that come into my practice. The other products did okay, however, I am completely sold on the **Separation Ease** Essence, since I used a bottle at the annual Canine Corp Day where veterinarians volunteer their services on police, narcotic, bomb, search and rescue dogs. I would spray the essence as the dogs entered the facility and I was amazed at how calm it made these dogs. Some of the dogs are notorious for not being able to be examined and this year, one in particular got examined at all of the stations. To say the least, my ears were not ringing by the time I left as there was very little barking between the working dogs. The director of the event asked me what I did to calm the dogs down because she has never seen the event run so smoothly. I told her I sprayed them with an essence and applied lavender to their "third eye." I am currently using **Separation Ease** on a dog that usually has seizures during storms and it has been working beautifully. Best product ever!*"

Dr. Gwendolyn Steffen, DVM Henehan Animal Hospital Milford, OH

Homework

Use your dedicated session connection time and location to connect with your animal for the intention of calming.

In Your Animal Connection and Healing session:

1. Prepare yourself with grounding, clearing, getting present, and protection from Chapter 2.

2. Prepare your environment with the steps from Chapter 3.

3. Prepare your cat/dog with grounding, clearing, and protecting from Chapter 4.

4. Practice the calming techniques from this chapter.

5. Take notice of your animal's responses with each calming technique.

6. Notice which ones felt more calming to you.

7. Notice which ones your animal seemed to like best and showed signs of calming.

8. Notice if they were the same techniques or different ones that you each responded to the most.

Celebrate! Calming is another foundational step that will support you going forward.

Post your experience with your Animal Connection and Healing session on the Healing You, Healing Your Animal Facebook group.

In this chapter you learned calming techniques, getting you into a more hands-on healing session with your animal. In the next chapter you will learn techniques to strengthen your intuition. This will help you feel more confident with the information you receive and strengthen it. It is like a muscle, the more you use it, the stronger it gets. Let's get started...

CHAPTER 6

Strengthening Intuition

MY INTENTION IS TO FOR YOU to gain clarity and strengthening of your intuition to help you deepen your connection with your animals.

Please know this is a journey. This may be the beginning or you may have already started on this journey. No matter where you are on your awareness of your intuition, this chapter will help you get stronger. This topic is much bigger than one chapter in this book. So be patient with yourself. It is like a muscle. The more you use it, the stronger it will become. And I am excited you are here working with your intuition.

Healing Activation: Intuition

Take a moment and close your eyes. If you are unable to close your eyes, pretend or imagine you can.

As you are going inward for a moment, see yourself sitting on a rock out in nature. It is a nice, fall day, with the wind slightly blowing through your hair. As you are feeling yourself connected to this rock below you and your feet on the earth, take a look around. Take a moment to notice the sky, and notice the grass, notice the trees. Notice if there are mountains. Imagine you see a butterfly coming to you, gently flying around you. You smile and receive a blessing of transformation coming to you. The butterfly is helping you open your awareness to your surroundings. It is the spark of intuition fluttering into your awareness. Feel this spark in your heart. Feel this light shining and extending down into your root chakra and extending more brightly up into your sixth chakra – your third eye – your center of intuition. As this light is emanating, awakening and preparing for heightened awareness right now, and the rest of your day, you are confident in the knowing that you will receive exactly what you are meant to receive with your intuition today. It is as calm as sitting on a rock, just being and noticing.

You can open your eyes.

As we are diving deeper with energy today, there is a key concept to take in:

ALL THINGS ARE CONNECTED

Everything is connected to everything else. Every person is connected to every other person. Every event is linked to those of the past and to those of the future. Everything relates to everything else. This is known as the Law of Correspondence. There is no such thing as coincidence. Every action has a reaction. Everything we do and think sets energy in motion and shapes what will unfold somewhere within our life. If we do one thing, something else will result from it.

The difficulty is figuring out how things relate. Sometimes the connections will be obvious. Other times, though, it takes a great deal of effort before we figure out these connections or why things happen the way they do.

I am here to let you know that no matter how far you are on opening your intuition, there is still fear and doubt that comes in. It is a matter of recognizing it and managing it.

When there is doubt and fear, focus on love. Fear cannot exist when love is present.

Take a moment now to connect with deep love. What helps you be in a loving state? As an animal lover, you probably are in a loving state when you think about your cat, your dog or other animal. Now that you have this loving feeling, remember to come back to this when you are feeling doubt, fear or confusion. Then you'll be ready to keep learning, strengthening and building your intuition.

Now it is time to go into how energy is sent and received.

There are the five physical senses you are familiar with eyes, ears, touch, nose, and mouth. There are energetic senses or "clairs" that correlate with the five physical senses, and an additional clair associated with faith. You can easily relate to your five physical senses because you use them every day. Here is more information to understand your energetic clairs that you are using and may or may not even realize it.

Eyes — Vision — Clairvoyance

Clairvoyance means clear seeing. You see with your physical eyes what is around you physically. You have the clair of clairvoyance that you may or may not be in tune with, where you see things with your mind's eye, also called your Third Eye and Sixth Chakra. When you imagine something, you see it like a movie playing in your forehead, you see colors and images much like a daydream and receive information that way. When you are highly visual, you best understand information when it is written down, in charts, sketches, drawings, photographs and the computer screen.

Ears — Hearing — Clairaudience

Clairaudience means clear hearing. You hear sounds with your physical ears. You have the clair of clairaudience that you may or may not be in tune with, where you hear things that are not around you physically. You hear words, sounds, or music in your mind in your own voice. When you are highly attuned to hearing, you best retain information when you hear it spoken aloud.

Touch — Feeling — Clairsentient

Clairsentient means clear feeling. You feel sensations with physical touch. You have the clair of clairsentience that you may or may not be in tune with, where you feel things that are not touching you physically. When you are highly sensitive, you feel what others around you are feeling. You get a "gut" reaction when someone walks in the room even though you have never met them. You get an overwhelming sense of love or resonance with someone you just met.

Nose — Smell — Clairalience

Clairalience means clear smelling.

You smell scents that aren't really there physically such as a scent of an orange, a rose, a pine tree, or something else that is information coming through from a source such as Spirit or your animal.

Mouth — Taste — Clairgustance

Clairgustance means clear tasting.

You may get a taste that is out of the blue because you are not physically eating something. That taste is information. You are receiving information through taste from Spirit or your animal.

Faith — Knowing — Claircognizance

Claircognizance means clear knowing.

There is a knowing, you just know, you don't how you know, you just know something to the core of your being as truth.

Claircognizance requires tremendous faith because you don't have a physical explanation of how you know what you know. You just do know and are certain.

Now you can expand your awareness with the energetic clairs you have available. Awareness is the first step and then you can strengthen them as you would a muscle.

Here's an exercise to help you strengthen your clairs.

Determine Your Predominant Clairs Exercise

Begin by sitting in a comfortable place where you won't be distracted or disturbed for a few minutes. Take a look and scan the area around you, taking in all details and feelings of your environment.

Now close your eyes and focus on your breath.

Breathe deeply and slowly as you mentally review what caught your attention when you scanned the room. Was it the sight of something that stood out, the sound of something that you heard, the feeling of something registering in your stomach (gut) or heart, a taste or smell that suddenly appeared, or a strong thought about something that came to you from out of the blue?

Open your eyes.

Now, take a look around and see if the room looks different in any way. Is the sun shining through brighter than it was? Is your cat or dog lying in a place they don't normally? Is something new catching your eye, coming into your awareness?

Write down what sense or senses were predominant in this exercise. This is key information on how you receive information and what to pay attention to when more information comes to you. The more you use your energetic clairs, the stronger they will be for you.

Once you are aware of the different ways your intuition and Spirit can speak to you, a door is opened to this powerful guidance, which will assist you in creating a meaningful and magical spiritual journey.

Homework

Be in nature in whatever way you enjoy. Take a nature walk, sit outside, sit with a plant, go to a plant store and walk around. (I find it better outside; however, with weather changing, do what you can for where you are). Go with an open mind (no expectations). In your intention, ask for clear signs to help you.

1. Set your intention before your walk.

2. Ask for guidance on a particular issue.

3. Be open to receive signs and answers in nature.

   (The events and observations that are unusual, out of context of normal patterns or not part of your daily contact will have the most significance to you.)

4. Stay objective – alignment with Source will always be true and accurate. If you are attached to the outcome, it can alter your responses since the information is coming from ego instead of Source.

5. When in doubt, ground and clear yourself.

6. Signs are sometimes subtle and sometimes they are very blatant and clear, and a whole range in between. For example, a subtle sign is similar to the exercise we did above, where you scanned the room and determined what you noticed, and something catches your attention as soon as you ask the question. You may see something out of the ordinary, or your animal will do something that you notice being different or you might see a literal sign, a window sign, a street sign or something answering your question. If you have seen the movie, "*Bruce Almighty*," do you remember the scene where he was asking God for a sign? He was desperately seeking a sign as he was passing street signs that he didn't see and a truck of signs pulled in front of him, very blatant, and he still didn't see them. (He was receiving answers with the signs; yet he wasn't seeing them.) You are on the lookout, so you will have a much better chance of seeing your signs. An example of a clear, blatant sign is when I was soul searching and I looked up in the sky to see the only cloud in the sky separate into three clouds and each cloud formed a letter, spelling the word JOY across the sky, clearly showing the message for me. This was early on when I was starting to ask a question and look to nature for a sign so I was feeling doubt, "Am I really seeing this? Did this really just happen?" And the answer is: Yes. Now, things like this happen all of the time with me so I know it is possible for you. Be open and see what shows up for you.

7. Post your experience with your session on the Healing You, Healing Your Animal Facebook group!

Remember, listening to your intuition is like a muscle, the more you use it, the stronger it gets. You can come back to this chapter and exercise for more practice.

Celebrate! You have received another foundational step supporting you with your animals going forward.

In this chapter, you learned techniques to strengthen your intuition, getting you into more awareness with how you send and receive information. Your animals send and receive information in this same way. This will help you with your Animal Connection and Healing sessions.

In the next chapter, you will learn Communicating with Your Animals.

Ready? Set? Let's Go...

CHAPTER 7

Communicating with Your Animals

MY INTENTION IS TO PROVIDE a very powerful chapter that helps you gain deeper understanding with communicating with your animals.

Healing Activation: Communicating with Your Animals

Take a moment and close your eyes. If you are not at a place where you can close your eyes, pretend or imagine you can. As you are closing your eyes, I invite you to come and be present now. Whatever has already been happening in your day can be put aside. It can wait outside the door and it and whatever else needs your attention will be there when you are finished with this chapter. This is a gift you are giving yourself not only for yourself, but for your animals as well.

Now I invite you to take a deep breath in, hold it, let it out. As your breath is cleansing and clearing, paving the way for you to relax, be more in this moment. Let's take another deep breath in, hold it, let it out. And as you are relaxing, letting go, and being here more fully, let's take another deep breath in, hold it and let it go. As you return to normal breathing, feel your breaths swirling through your physical body and integrating; notice how your body feels. Are you more open? Are you able to breathe in more fully? More deeply? Just notice, no judgment.

Imagine you are sitting in an open, grassy field on a sunny day with light clouds, a slight breeze, and you are very comfortable. There are trees in the distance, there are birds flying in the air, butterflies flittering from one wildflower to the next wildflower. You are there with your animal in an open field of delightful play. As you are sitting there enjoying your day, take a moment and...

Visual

Take a look around. What do you see? Are there trees? If so, what color are the leaves? Do you see wildflowers? What color are they? What size are they? Are they large, medium, small? Are they short or tall? Take notice of what all you see. What color is the grass you are sitting on?

Feeling

Now, take a moment to feel the grass underneath you. Is it thick and soft, or is it sparse and coarse? What texture is it? What thickness is it? Reach out and touch a flower. Does it have a lot of petals or a few? Are the petals soft and smooth? Or something else? Now there is a butterfly coming and gently landing in your open hand. Take a moment and feel how soft its touch is. As the butterfly takes a few steps on your hand, notice the sensation, are they light and delicate or heavy steps? Does it tickle when it walks?

Smell

Now take a deep breath in and take in the scents around you. What do you notice? The fresh scents of the flowers, the freshness in the air. What smells are there for you? No right or wrong, notice what you sense and smell.

Taste

Now turn your attention to your mouth. Is there a taste that comes to you? Imagine you brought along your favorite fruit. Take a bite. How does it taste? Is it sweet, sour, watery, dry, course or smooth, pulpy or slippery? Savor it as you are chewing it. Really activate your sense of taste.

Hear

Now put your attention on your ears. What sounds are you hearing around you? Are you hearing any sounds? Are you hearing birds chirping? Are you hearing an ocean in the background? Are you so still and the silence is so clear you sense it is possible to hear the butterfly flapping its wings? Notice what shows up here for you.

Knowing

As you are in this field, check in and see if there is a "knowing" for you. Is there a sense of knowledge that feels so right to you? It is so clear to you even though you don't know how you know it, others may not understand it, and that doesn't really matter. What is important is that you know this to your core and feel good about it.

With all of your senses open, now see your cat or dog coming to sit next to you in this field. You have a conversation. Your dog is telling you something he/she wants you to know.

Your senses are open, you listen, you receive and you communicate back to him/her where you both understand each other. The lines of communication are open between the two of you. You sit here lovingly connected for your entire conversation. You embrace this joyful clear connection and conversation.

Take a deep breath in, hold it, let it out.

Your conversation comes to a close. You hug each other and you are ready to leave the field. You each are grateful for this connection and know there will be many more.

Take a deep breath in, hold it, let it out.

Wiggle your hands. Wiggle your feet.

When you are ready, **open your eyes.**

Communicating

Your animals have multiple ways of communicating with you. The key is being open to receive this information.

Your animals have body language that gives you a lot of information by watching them. They use their eyes, ears, mouth, tail and body posture to communicate. They also communicate with pictures, feelings, taste, smell and hearing. And in a healing session, they also may direct their session by rolling over and presenting the part of their body for you to work with first before going on to another part. Animals have an innate connection and knowing with their body and they listen to it. So trust them.

When communicating with your animals, it is important to express what you desire your animal to do. As a human, you are more prone to tell your animals what you don't want. It is how your brain works and it is so prevalent in our society. So it takes some practice, awareness and re-training on your part to be able to consistently focus on the positive rather than the negative.

Animals do not know the word "no." So anytime you put the word "no" in front of something, you are actually telling them to do it. You are sending them the picture of it and that is what they see, hear and feel.

As a human, when you see a sign with cell phone wrapped with a big red circle and a big red line across it, you see the cell phone and then translate the "no" to add to it – reading it as "no cell phones here." Animals do not have this capability. What they see is the cell phone. The big red circle with the line across it has no meaning to them. So they think the picture you send is what you want them to do.

For example, telling your dogs – "Don't jump on the couch." This statement sends them a visual. The visual you are sending is the couch with a big red circle around it with a big red line through it. All they see is you talking about the couch and them jumping on the couch. The "no" or "don't" has no meaning in their language. So, they jump on the couch thinking they are doing well, this is what you want, this is what you are telling them, and they are very pleased with themselves. And they are very confused when they get into trouble. And you are frustrated when your dog keeps jumping on the couch when you think you are saying not to. So you get stressed that they aren't listening to you. In their minds, they are listening to you and don't understand why you are so mad. So you can see and feel the confusion and tension in this scenario.

To alleviate this from happening, think in terms of what you do want your animals to do. And then ask them to do that.

Using the couch example again – if your dog jumps on the couch, say what you would like him/her to do. "Stay on the floor," "sit on your rug," "lie on your bed," all the while visualizing your dog where you desire him/her to be.

We'll take this one step deeper. You picture your couch empty with no one on it. You visualize your dog walking in front of the couch with all four paws staying on the floor and the couch still being empty. This sends the clear message to your dog, the couch stays free of him/her.

Pay attention to your words this week with your animals. Listen for how many times you tell your animals "no." For instance, I hear this a lot: "no bark." Your dog does not understand this clearly. You are actually telling him/her to bark with your words and your body language is telling him/her you are upset. So your dog gets stressed and out of sorts, not being sure what you really want him/her to do and he/she will more likely bark even more.

Another one I hear a lot is "no teeth" for puppy teething and chewing. You can shift this to "chew on the ball," "chew on this toy," or "good chew on toy," as you are removing your hand, showing and giving him/her the toy.

These may sound so obvious here, but for some this may be new. As humans, it is so ingrained to speak in terms of "no" and what you do not want, that you usually aren't aware you are doing it.

I invite you to pay attention to when you are saying NO and how often.

Also, do you use the phrase, "no, don't do <fill in the blank>." For instance "no, don't jump on the couch," "no, don't chase after that dog," "no, don't...."

I invite you to pay attention to when you are using "no, don't" and how often.

Do you use the words "bad dog" when your dog does something you do not like? Or say "bad cat?" This works the same for cats and dogs. I invite you to reframe this to thinking about bad behavior versus bad animal. This will shift the energy greatly for your animal.

I invite you to pay attention to when you are saying "bad dog," "bad cat," and how often.

In my practice, I support animals with this kind of clarity. The animals are feeling sheepish and uncertain, because in their minds they have done something wrong that disappointed their human, yet they are unclear what it is. And when I ask the person, sometimes they don't recall what it was, yet their animal is still carrying it around. After we clear it, the animal feels good again, with more confidence and zest.

Something to keep in mind is that thoughts are energy. So even thinking about not wanting your dog to jump on the couch sends the picture to your dog to jump on the couch. Remember the big red circle around the cell phone earlier? This is sending the picture of the big red circle around your couch message to your dog. You don't have to even speak it for your animals to get the message. This is where the retraining of how you think and speak about the way you desire things to be. Focus on the actions for your animals to take versus what you do not want to happen with your animals.

The concept that thoughts are energy applies to names, too. Pay attention to your animal's name or nickname. If your animal is being called "little monster," guess what? That is what you are telling your animal to be. So his/her behavior will continue being the "little monster." Name and nickname your animals with loving names, showing them respect, and you will receive loving behavior with them.

So far you have been discovering how animals receive information. The next section is about how you will receive information from your animals when they are speaking with you.

The way animals speak to us is not the same as you and I talking with each other. Their language is in pictures, sounds, feelings, taste and knowingness – the clairs.

Stay open, because the more you are unattached to the answer, the clearer it will be.

Vickie and Desi

Vickie first came to me when she was concerned with Desi competing in agility. She wants to be a responsible dog guardian and wondered if the competitions were too taxing on Desi's body.

Desi was getting older and was having some back leg tremors, so she needed some support to continue competing. As a private client, Desi received massage, acupressure and Reiki, along with using Healing Your Animal **Pain Ease** and **Muscle Ease** essences. Desi felt better and these essences significantly reduced her leg tremors. Desi went on to achieve her North American Dog Agility Council (NADAC)

Agility Trial Champion title, feeling good and still doing agility a year later.

Desi likes being a star and the center of attention. She is happy being featured on the front and back cover of this book.

Vickie and August

Vickie had a great experience taking my Animal Connection and Healing Group with August, another dog. August was not like any of her other dogs she has had, so Vickie took the Animal Connection and Healing Group to understand him better. August was a clear communicator in his way. He danced to the beat of his own drum as the saying goes. Vickie was learning to tune into listening to what August was sharing. In one instance, Vickie was so frustrated that she was asking August a question and all she was getting was the color red. (By the way, Vickie was turning red with frustration thinking August was not cooperating with her.) August was answering her question. August really loved the grounding. Red is the color of the root chakra, Chakra 1, which is all about grounding, safety, and security. August was sharing with Vickie that he wanted her to do grounding with him. When Vickie understood that August was communicating with her, it was a turning point in opening their connection, communication and their relationship. August has two NADAC titles and is really teaming up with Vickie better now in their agility runs. Before this group, August was barking and going after other dogs. It was very chaotic and unsettling — August was unmanageable. As a result of the new grounding and connection, August is able to go to places like Canon Beach with the family where Vickie can relax and have fun with August being calmer.

Before you try to communicate with your animals, ask yourself, "Am I open? Am I connected to Spirit/Source/Universe/Higher Guidance?" If yes, then proceed. If not, ground and clear yourself and ask again until you are connected. Next ask yourself, "Do I have an attachment to the answer?" If yes, stop, slow down, clear and open and check again. As long as you have an attachment to the answer (really wanting it to be one way) you will not get a clear answer.

It is about knowing yourself and being honest – asking, "Am I open to Source?" Or, "Am I attached to my ego?" When you are expanded, open, and in flow, you are connected to Source. When you are constricted, constrained, stressed, worried, and doubting, you are in ego and not open to a clear Source answer.

When a thought or image comes to mind and you wonder, "Where in the world did this come from? Am I making it up?" That is a big clue to stop and check in. Is your energy open to Source flowing? Do you have an open heart, are you connected to your feelings, or are you in your head, connected to thoughts and ego? Are you attached to the information? Is this something your mind normally has for you? Or is it different?

When you receive a clear yes/no that boosts your confidence, you can ask, "Is it coming from me?" (If the answer is "yes," then it isn't coming from Source or the animal, so ignore it.) Is it coming from the cat/dog/animal you are working with? (If the answer is "yes," pay attention.) Is it coming from Source? (If the answer is "yes," pay attention.)

Sometimes as an animal guardian, you may be inclined to make assumptions about your cat/dog and what they are already thinking and communicating to you. And vice versa, you may think you are communicating clearly to your animal. Sometimes what we communicate isn't taken clearly by our animal. I know firsthand, because my cat, Tasha, taught me. Tasha was 14 at this time and had lived with me since being adopted from the pound at seven weeks old. She had been with me through moving and transitions a number of times in our time together. So when I was packing boxes and moving for the next venture at this stage in my life, Tasha started acting funny. I got concerned and reached out to an animal communicator friend. She was very frank with me and said Tasha doesn't know she is going with you in your move. I exclaimed "What? Of course she is coming with me!" My friend said "Yes, you know this, but she doesn't know it. You haven't told her." Wow, was I taken aback. I had not realized I hadn't told her even though it was certainly clear to me she was coming too. Once I shared this news with Tasha that she indeed was coming with me, she was much calmer and happier.

With your animals and communication, sometimes the information is literal and clear and sometimes you need a symbol, idea, or feeling to get the information across. The more open you are to this, the easier it will be to decipher the message. And the more you do it, the easier it gets. Be patient; it takes time and this is a journey and progression you are on with your cat/dog.

Laura and Ginger

Remember Laura and Ginger from Chapter 2? When taking the Animal Connection and Healing Group, Laura really received and practiced these techniques that you are reading now in this book. Each week Ginger kept improving and improving and improving. By now, Laura's immediate family, extended family and even her neighbors were commenting on the change in Ginger. Ginger was much calmer. She wasn't going after the neighbors. She wasn't barking like crazy at every move and every one. Ginger was able to go camping and stayed calm around other dogs. Ginger is now much happier and more content.

Homework

In your dedicated special connection time with your cat and dog this week:

1. Pay attention to when you use the word "no" and the phrase "don't do ..." or together "no, don't do..." And start reframing the ideas into what you do want your animal to actually do.

2. Pick something you would like to tell your animal to do differently. (You can start small to help success be quicker and easier for you. And then build up to bigger things.)

3. An example you can begin with is when your dog barks every time a person or animal walks by outside. Even though this gets on your nerves, say in a calm voice "thank you." "Thank you for letting me know." Then say "go watch." Visualize in your mind a picture of watching quietly as the person or animal walks by. This is the new behavior you desire.

4. I was walking around a neighborhood on the road when a Boston Terrier was standing at the end of his driveway barking and barking and barking. As I was passing him I said "good protecting, what a good job you are doing." He got this perplexed look on his face and sat down quietly. It was clear to me he was saying "Oh my gosh, she understood me."

5. Post your experiences on the Healing You, Healing Your Animal Facebook group. I look forward to seeing them!

Remember to be patient with yourself. Intuition and communication are like muscles, the more you use them, the stronger they get. And train yourself to communicate to your animals what you desire them to do.

Celebrate! You have received another foundational step supporting you and your animals communicating and having a deeper bond together.

In this chapter you learned about communicating with your animals.

In the next chapter you will learn the importance of assigning your cat/dog a role. This will help you have harmony in your household. Ready? Set? Role...

CHAPTER 8

Importance of Roles

My intention is to provide a very powerful chapter that helps you understand and establish roles with your animals.

Healing Activation

Let's take a moment and get centered. Set aside all that has been going on in your day, knowing you can pick up what is there for you when you get done, and what you are ready to let go of can go on its way. I invite you to gently close your eyes.

Now take a deep breath in, hold it, let it out. Now take another deep breath in, hold it, let it out. And now for the power of three, take another deep breath in, hold it, let it out. As you breathe normally, I invite you to imagine or sense you and your animals. And if you have multiple animals, you can see each of them in the room. I invite you to open and receive the information that is yours to receive at this time.

Check in with your animal(s), ask to be given or shown who they are. What is their temperament or their personality? What is something that stands out about each of them?

Start with one of them and go through each one individually. As you are seeing what really stands out about them, they are beaming. They are highlighted on a stage lit up with a spotlight on them and you can really see them. You can really see them acting and being who they are, what they love to do; take notice. What are you seeing? Who are they? How are they here to help you? And what do you see that they contribute to the household? You thank them. Now if you have another animal, invite your next animal up on stage. You see the crowd applauding and they are beaming with a smile, they are performing and doing what they normally do. You can really see your animal(s) and the actions that they are doing. You really get a good look at them and what really brings them to life. Really take that in, deepening your connection and having these characteristics come forward so you can continue to praise them.

So now if you have more animals in your household, I invite you to take a moment and see each one coming up on stage, really seeing who they are, connecting and grasping the feeling of them. So when you have each of your animal's characteristics, their uniqueness, their specialness, I invite you to go up to each one, give them a hug, and thank them for being them. And as you interact with each one of your animals, both of you are beaming in that moment, really connecting. Now go to your next animal, acknowledging and hugging them. Really see them in their greatness, their fullness. Continue to go to each of your animals, give them a hug and thank them for who they are. Continue this until you have gone through all of your animals.

Now see yourself connected in a circle and you are holding paws and hands, forming a strong family unit of harmony and connection and appreciation for one another. You are all filling your circle with love, an abundance of love and respect and really seeing each other for who you are. In this circle, you all acknowledge your differences, and really appreciate your family connection.

When you are ready, you can open your eyes.

Roles are a very necessary and integral part of living with your animals.

Establishing roles is extremely important in a household with multiple animals.

Your animals love you so much, they naturally do things to "help" you. If the roles are not assigned, sometimes your cat/dog will assign their roles naturally to themselves and it isn't always in their best interest for their overall health. Then they start not doing well. You start to get worried, which then upsets them and a vicious cycle starts between the two of you, taking up a lot of energy and concern and health issues for both you and your animals.

Households with multiple animals where the animals do not have assigned roles generally have a lot of conflict between the animals. They will each try to position themselves closest to you and be the most helpful.

So it is a very important step to assign roles to each of the animals in your household.

Some common roles are:

- Protector/guardian of your house
- Protector/guardian of you
- Overseer of Household (different than protector)
- Jester/keeping you lightened up with laugh and play
- Greeter
- Lapwarmer/Bed, Couch or Chair Snuggler

Your animals are doing something naturally, so their role has been happening already. You can refine this by turning it into an official role, so your animals are doing what they naturally do and now you are making it official so they receive praise for it. This goes a long way in curbing behaviors you don't desire. And most importantly, they feel important and special. This will minimize "acting out" and jealousy between multiple animal members in your household. This is the same for cats and for dogs, and households with both cats and dogs. Everyone gets a role. Everyone is clear about their roles, proud doing them, and happy receiving praise for doing them.

In Chapter 2 you met Pablo with Sally benefiting from grounding.

Here is more of their story:

When Sally first came to me, she was in tears thinking she had made a mistake adopting Pablo and bringing another cat into her home because of the disruption it caused Vincent. Vincent was more shy by nature and Pablo was bullying Vincent.

"I was dealing with constant stress because our two cats, Vincent and Pablo, weren't getting along. Pablo was very dominant and aggressive, and Vincent, who's very shy, would spend the whole day hiding, living in constant isolation and fear. Since I've been working with Vicki, the whole mood of our household has changed. Vincent is much more confident than he used to be, and it's clear that he's more at ease and happy in the house. Pablo is less of a bully and is starting to use more of his energy for playing and enjoying life vs. negative behavior. I even see the two cats sleeping together and grooming each other occasionally. I feel much more relaxed and productive during the day as I'm not constantly worried about the boys, and I'm confident leaving them alone together when I have to travel." Sally McKenzie, Seattle, WA

Some animals have one role and that role is very important.

Sometimes animals can have more than one role. It is important that the roles are different with each of your animals when you have more than one animal in the household. This keeps things clear between you and your animals. It enables each animal to true be special in their role. Your animals take pride in their roles.

In taking the Animal Connection and Healing Group to further support Vincent and Pablo, Sally discovered that establishing roles was a missing link for the harmony in the household.

Vincent likes being called King Vincent. He is the love cat. He is the lap cat. He spreads love throughout the household. He is a snuggler and a big brother. He has come a long way from being a private client and participating in the group. Vincent did come out to the middle of the room during the photo shoot. (This was a miracle for him to come out with strangers in his house, especially one with a big camera). It was too much for him to stay out and get a good photo for you to enjoy. But we were so proud of him for his accomplishment.

Pablo is the play cat, the jester. He thinks everything is a game. He's also an athlete with his many jumps, a hunter protecting the house from pests, a little brother and the entertainer of the household.

Once we established the roles for Vincent and Pablo, Vincent came to the phone during class, purring loudly and rubbing the phone as a thank you. Sally shared that this was so out of character for Vincent. This was an endearing moment that Vincent stepped forward and shared.

Sharing the story of Lynn and her dog family will give you a good example of assigning roles and how, as life changes, your animals' roles change.

Tusk was with Lynn for 11 years. He was the lead dog in the household, Lynn's protector and the healing dog for the family. When I say healing, Tusk was Reiki Master-attuned.

Lynn and X

As a Reiki Master Teacher, I find that some of my animal clients benefit from receiving a Reiki attunement. The Reiki attunement raises the vibration of the animal, which supports them with their own self-healing. In my experience, a Reiki attunement when the animal is very sick often shifts them to a path of healing and recovery. When it is the animal's time to pass, the attunement assists the animal with natural pain relief, easing the time of transition. And there are a few animals dedicated to take on the healing role of healing others on a bigger scale and receive the Reiki Master attunement, such as Tusk.

Tusk shared a household with Derby, X and Candy.

Derby was Tusk's daughter and also a Reiki Master. Reiki Masters have many roles and have a variety of personalities. Derby's first love was always children. As a Reiki Master, she took on the role of helping Lynn to teach children and their dogs. She healed other dogs who were working with their children who had previous traumatic experiences. She also had the role of lead playmate for Lynn's nephews and niece, healing and protecting them.

X and Candy are Tusk's grand puppies. He is a proud grandpa.

Tusk taught X how to protect Lynn and taught Candy how to protect Alexis and how to be lead dog for all of the dogs in the household. Alexis is Lynn's niece who lives with her. She was 8 at the time Candy was born. Candy became Alexis' protector.

Alexis and Candy

While Tusk was alive, X was the puppy that wanted to be just like grandpa, so he focused on being the student to the master. X knew he would grow up to be the master healer and protector of the household and that he had some big paws to fill. X would watch and imitate Tusk. One day Lynn had brought both of them in for Tusk's appointment. I walked into the room and looked at X. My first impression was that he was Tusk. Then I looked over and Tusk was there. Lynn laughed and told me that X had been busy practicing to be just like Tusk. He was doing a good job energetically that day.

Lynn and X

When Tusk transitioned, X took over the role of Lynn's protector and main support dog. His role includes guarding and
protecting Lynn. X is also Reiki Master-attuned and he took
over being the healing dog and keeping everything balanced
in the household.

Alexis and Candy

Candy's role is still being responsible for Alexis, now 16 years old. Candy helps Alexis with everything and is Alexis' protector. With Tusk's transition, Candy took on the role of being the lead for all the dogs in the household.

It came time to add a new addition to the dog family. Introducing Hattie, X's daughter...

Lynn and Hattie

Hattie is now the young one and her role is the puppy. She entertains Lynn's family with her puppy antics and makes sure they all understand her puppy love.

As you can see, when life changes, when animals transition and new animals come into your household, the roles shift.

Pay attention when something shifts in your household and keep roles current with your cats and your dogs.

I have facilitated and witnessed numerous households with multiple animals shift from chaos and lots of frustration to harmony and calm when roles were established, assigned, and then rewarded with praise. This **shifted from** all of the animals spending energy, scrambling to be seen and heard, vying to fulfill household needs and being out-of-sorts **to** each animal being responsible for his/her part, and each animal being clear about his/her role. So each animal is now specifically focused, and the household energies are very harmonious with very happy animals and very happy people.

You read about Niko and Levi in Chapter 4. Levi is where the role of "Jester" got created for my clients and my teachings. He is a true jester and does his job well.

It is very important to stay open and be mindful of all of your animals performing their role, no matter what else is going on in your life, as Levi showed us. He continued to be playful and doing his job as Sheri was very sad and helping Niko as he was going through his end-of-life journey. With Sheri honoring Levi doing his job in the midst of the sadness, Levi was part of the process. He was involved and an important part of the family. Sheri could tend to Niko, knowing Levi was there too.

Remember in Chapter 7 we discussed how names are energy and to be mindful of what you call your animal? This goes for assigning roles too. My cat, Tyler, was the only male in the household of three cats (two female) and myself. I would joke around and call him the "Man of the House." When it came time for him to transition from this life, he kept holding on. He was getting weaker and weaker and I was giving him permission to transition. Then it dawned on me. He was hanging on, fulfilling his role of "Man of the House." There was not another man to take his place, so he was hanging on to living. When I realized this, I shared with him I was going to be okay. I took him to the vet to support him transitioning. As Tyler's spirit left his body, he encircled me with a big energetic hug and was so delighted for his spirit to be free. I was grateful for this experience, knowing I did the right thing.

Homework

In your dedicated special connection time for you and your animal this week...

Assign your cat/dog a role. (Assign all of the animals in your household a role.) You can "talk" to them about it. You can literally use your voice and words to tell them their role. (You will also be giving them pictures with your thoughts, so they will clearly understand their role.) Praise them for all they have done up to now. This is setting you both up for a closer relationship.

I invite you to post your experiences on the Healing You, Healing Your Animal Facebook group.

Celebrate! You have received another foundational step, supporting you and your animals communicating and having a deeper bond together.

In this chapter you learned about assigning roles with your animals. This will help you with your Animal Connection and Healing sessions.

In the next chapter you will learn how to put it all together. Ready? Set... Let's go!

CHAPTER 9

Putting It All Together

Wow, what a journey we have been on. We are now putting it all together into an Animal Connection and Healing session.

First let's set intentions. My intention is for you to have very successful Animal Connection and Healing sessions with your animal(s) now and going forward. This chapter helps you embrace clarity on all the things you have learned so far. Know that you can come back to this book to take your learning deeper with each read and use of these techniques. You have a good foundational understanding and connection with your animals. And this has helped broaden the connection and healing journey you're on with your animal(s).

Healing Activation: Grounding Cord Exercise

Take a moment and close your eyes. If you are not at a place where you can close your eyes, pretend or imagine you can.

As you are closing your eyes, I invite you to come and be present. Whatever has already been happening in your day can be put aside. It can wait outside the door and it and whatever else needs your attention will be there when you are finished. This is a gift you are giving yourself; not only for yourself, for your animals as well.

Now I invite you to take a deep breath in, hold it, let it out. As your breath is cleansing and clearing, paving the way for you to relax, be more in this moment. Let's take another deep breath in, hold it, let it out. And as you are relaxing, letting go, and being here more fully in this moment, let's take another deep breath in, hold it and let it go.

As you return to normal breathing, feel your breaths swirling through your physical body and integrating; notice how your body feels. Is it more open, are you able to breathe in more fully, more deeply? Notice what is going on in your body and mind, just notice, no judgment.

I invite you to put your puppies (your ego worries and doubts) in their basket over to the side.

Chakra 1 is the Root Chakra. It is located at the base of your spine and its color is red. It is closest to the earth with the densest frequency. It represents survival and safety.

Place your hands on your lower pelvic region. See your grounding cord coming out from the center of your root chakra (base of your spine) and going down through the floor, through the Earth, all the way down to the center of the Earth. If you are unable to see or feel this, pretend or imagine you can. You are taking the end of it and pulling it down, all the way down to the center of the Earth. Wrap your grounding cord around the core/center of the Earth. There is a ball of light, a core of light. So keep going down deep until you reach this light.

Now imagine you have roots coming out of the soles of your feet. These roots are going deep into the Earth. The roots are going all the way down to the center of the Earth. Now you have a tripod of stability and grounding connecting to the center of the Earth. These roots are flexible. You can walk, run, jump, play, climb and still be totally grounded and connected to the Earth.

The light from the center of the Earth is coming up your grounding cord into your root chakra.

Imagine your root chakra is cleansing and clearing all that is no longer needed and allowing in the energy of a balanced healthy root chakra.

Take a deep breath in, hold it, let it out. Take another deep breath in, hold it, let it out. Now for the power of three, take another deep breath in, hold it, let it out. Now come back to normal breathing. Take a moment and check in. How are you feeling as these three deep breaths are swirling in your body? Allow yourself to be present and to be clear and ready for your session.

❧ *Your Essence Experience* ❧

*For extra support, use Healing You **Iceland Spar** essence. It is a simple, effective, easy-to-use way to center and get present. Simply spray the essence three times in the air around you to receive centering support.*

Chakra 2 is the Sacral Chakra. It is located two inches below your navel, and its color is orange. This chakra represents your sexuality, your creativity, birthing not only of a physical child, it is the birthing of new ideas and projects, the center of your creativity and passions.

Place your hands on your lower abdomen two inches below your navel. Imagine your sacral chakra is cleansing and clearing all that is no longer needed and allowing in the energy of a balanced, healthy sacral chakra.

Chakra 3 is the Solar Plexus Chakra. It is located between your bellybutton and the base of your rib cage, and its color is yellow. It is your center of power, center of will, it is how you present yourself into the world. It is also your center of manifestation, so when you state your desires and intentions into the world, they can be answered and delivered to you.

Place your hands on your abdomen above your navel and below your rib cage. Imagine your solar plexus chakra is cleansing and clearing all that is no longer needed and allowing in the energy of a balanced, healthy solar plexus chakra.

Chakra 4 is the Heart Chakra. It is located in the center of your chest, and its color is green. It is your center of love, unconditional love, and compassion. This is the connection with oneness with everyone, from your heart. This is a universal language of love, this goes for your animals, too. They know and sense this and connect on the heart level.

Place your hands on your chest. Imagine your heart chakra is cleansing and clearing all that is no longer needed and allowing in the energy of a balanced, healthy heart chakra.

Chakra 5 is the Throat Chakra. It is located in the center of your throat, and its color is sky blue. It is the center for speaking your truth, clarity of speaking, your voice, expressing your true self. You are speaking your truth, your dogs are barking, your cats are meowing – for purity of speech.

Place your hands on your throat. Imagine your throat chakra is cleansing and clearing all that is no longer needed and allowing in the energy of a balanced, healthy throat chakra.

Chakra 6 is the Third Eye Chakra. It is located in the center of your forehead, and its color is indigo blue. This is your center of intuition, your clarity, this is 360-degree vision.

As humans, a lot of the time we are "in our head." You may have heard the saying, "shift from your head to your heart" or "get grounded." As this chakra opens, it brings the energies from all of the mental activity down into your heart center and root chakra, opening your being to be connected with the present moment here on the Earth.

Place your hands on your forehead. Imagine your third eye chakra is cleansing and clearing all that is no longer needed and allowing in the energy of a balanced, healthy third eye chakra.

Chakra 7 is the Crown Chakra. It is located on the top of your head, and its color is light purple, or white with gold. This is your connection center to God, Source, Higher Power, Universe, whatever that term is to you. With this chakra open, you get crystal clear connection, guidance and support.

Place your hands on the top of your head. Imagine your crown chakra is cleansing and clearing all that is no longer needed and allowing in the energy of a balanced, healthy crown chakra.

You can place your hands wherever is now comfortable.

Imagine a white light (your protective bubble) circling your body about an arm's width out. It goes two feet above your head and two feet below your feet, forming a protective bubble of light around you.

Your protective bubble is semi-permeable. It allows love and good in and out of your energy field and keeps lower-level energies of others out.

You can open your eyes.

Go to your Animal Connection and Healing session spot and set up your space for your session.

    a. Clear the space

    b. Quiet your home phone

    c. Silence your cell phone

    d. Turn your TV off

    e. Turn away from your computer

    f. Turn away from your deadlines and to-do lists

    g. Play soft music

    h. Adjust lighting

Make it comfortable for you so it is comfortable for your animal.

Ground Your Animal

Place your hands on top of your animal's paw on the floor. Imagine sending energy down through your hand through your animal's paw and deep into the earth below the floor. This supports connecting your animal's paws to the ground to help him/her feel the grounding effect.

❧ Your Essence Experience ❧

*For extra support, use Healing Your Animal **Ground** essence. It is a simple, effective, easy-to-use way to ground your animal. Simply spray the essence three times in the air around you to receive grounding support.*

Clear Your Animal

Put on an imaginary energy protection glove – similar to putting on a glove to wash your dishes.

Place your hand two to four inches above your animal's body. Start with your hand over the nose and run your hand above your animal's body, down the center line all the way to the base of his/her tail. As you are doing this, envision collecting everything that is no longer needed from your animal's energy field into your hand as you make your pass from the nose, over the forehead, down the back of the head, over the shoulders, down the center of the back, over the hips, and out the base of the tail.

Once you have completed this, imagine you are flicking the energy off into an energy recycle bin to remove it from your hand, still with your glove on. Once you have discarded the collected energy, you can take off your energy protection glove. The intention is to let go of all of the energy no longer needed, what is ready to release, what isn't your animal's energy that he/she collected throughout his/her day. The intention is that his/her energy field is replenished with light, optimal health and healing, and vibrant energies.

⟨ Your Essence Experience ⟩

*For extra support, use Healing Your Animal **Clear** essence. It is a simple, effective, easy-to-use way to clear your animal's energy field. Simply spray the essence three times in the air around your animal to receive clearing support.*

Protect Your Animal

Now put a protective white bubble of light around your animal as you learned to do for yourself.

⟨ Your Essence Experience ⟩

*For extra support, use Healing Your Animal **Protection** essence. It is a simple, effective, easy-to-use way to protect your animal. Simply spray the essence three times in the air around you to receive protection support.*

Calming Techniques

Use the calming techniques you learned in Chapter 5, including:

- CV17 – center of chest

- Two-hand connection

- Using slow soothing voice

- Slowly rubbing bridge of nose

- Rubbing Ears

- Lightly holding hand over sacrum (low back)

- Include the center of chest with holding the low back

Communication

Is there a question you would like to ask your animal? Ask him/her now in your Animal Connection and Healing session.

Roles

Take a moment and check in with your animals' roles – is there clarity with your cats/dogs and their roles? Is something more ready to be shown to you? Ask that it be shown in a clear manner here.

Ask your animal if there is anything more that needs to be addressed? If so, take care of it before closing your session.

Close your session with gratitude.

Gratitude

Thank your animal for all he/she does for you.

Thank your space for supporting you with your animal for connection and healing.

Clear your space.

Homework Recommendation

Continue having and using your dedicated session connection time and location to connect with your animal for the intention of communicating, healing and receiving guidance on how to best support your precious loving cats and dogs.

If you desire the support of the Healing Your Animal essences, I invite you to order them here:

HealingYourAnimal.com/Products.php

Take a moment and check in... What has been the most memorable special shift/change/realization in connection with your animal while reading this book?

What do you see for your animal next?

For your animals, are you saying:

- Now that my dog isn't running away, I would really like to make sure he/she is able to run and move freely for many more years.

- Now that my cat(s) have clear roles and there is more harmony in my family, I would like to learn techniques to help my cat(s) look, feel and be their best.

- Now that I understand animals better and have learned some healing techniques, I would like to learn even more about how to help my dogs and cats heal behavioral issues and physical ailments.

Great!

I am so looking forward to continuing our work together, either one-on-one or in a group such as the one this book is modeled after. You can learn more advanced healing techniques in my upcoming book *Heart to Heart – How You Can Heal Your Animal.*

Vicki using healing touch with X

The day of the photo shoot X had a headache and he guided me to work with his head. He is such a great teacher. He was leading me to share this photo. You get a glimpse of what is coming in my next book, *Heart to Heart – How You Can Heal Your Animal.*

You are amazing and it has truly been an honor to be joined with you and your animals in support of having you and your animals be in optimum health, harmony, connection and peace.

This is Vicki Draper, Healing You, Healing Your Animal Expert.

Sending you many, many hugs with lots of love, purrs and woofs!

ABOUT THE AUTHOR

Vicki Draper with daughter Miranda and cats Spirit and Sapphire

Vicki Draper is a highly regarded modern-day animal healer and author who supports family animals with health, harmony and ease addressing wellness during every stage of your animal's life. With her skill set, she serves people locally and remotely, nationally and internationally.

She is featured in multiple books and magazines, and is the creator of healing products sold around the country and around the world. A natural-born animal communicator, Vicki's qualifications as a healer for both people and animals include being a licensed massage practitioner, a certified acupressurist and Reiki Master/Teacher, and training in craniosacral therapy.

Vicki lives in the Greater Seattle Area with her daughter, Miranda, and two cats, Spirit and Sapphire. She loves to walk in nature daily, connecting with herons, eagles and wildlife, bringing nature's wisdom into her life and healing practice.

If you would like further assistance with yourself or your animals, I invite you to schedule a Healing Your Animal Assessment where we discuss your issues and concerns and together determine the best plan of support.

Connect with Vicki at HealingYourAnimal.com

Made in the USA
San Bernardino, CA
04 June 2016